WALK WITH ME

By Argentine Imanirakunda
and Dawn Hurley

Dawn Hurley
dhurley@shonacongo.com
www.shonacongo.com

Publisher's Note: The events, places, and conversations in this memoir have been recreated from memory. Some events, individuals, and names have been omitted to respect the privacy of those involved. The name of Chantal was changed.

Walk With Me/Imanirakunda and Hurley -- 1st ed.
ISBN 979-8-218-600303

This book is a collaborative effort. It is based on Argentine's memories of her own childhood, and it was written in consultation with Argentine's mother, Uzamukunda Nababonye.

The conversations are recreated. The people and events are based on real people and events. Any changes from our first book are intentional. These changes reflect new input from Argentine's mother.

This is her story, too.

"And now these three remain: faith, hope and love. But the greatest of these is love."

1 Corinthians 13:13

PROLOGUE

You saw me the other day. I was at the grocery store on my motorized scooter, near the avocados that sell for two dollars each. My daughter was pushing the grocery cart, and her nose was running, because it is cold here in Canada.

"Argentine! Are you here on your own?" you asked, looking around the brightly lit aisles. I smiled and greeted you. But I wanted to tell you that I'm not on my own—even when I'm lost in this grocery store, looking for milk, thick and sour, like the kind we used to drink in Congo.

My mother lives in a refugee camp in Uganda, but every day she wakes in the dark to call me. I wanted to tell you about my mother and brothers and all my family. I wanted to tell you about my life in Congo, so you will know one thing for certain. I am not on my own—and neither are you.

But first, let me start from the beginning.

Part I

Faith

Chapter 1

Travel with me to the hills of Masisi—where the avocados fall fat from the trees. There are no grocery stores or motorized scooters. There is not even a road that leads to our village—only a footpath that turns to mud when it rains.

Walk left from Mweso, over the hill called Bushanga, through the swamp and the banana leaves covered in mist. Walk all day until you reach a house by the side of the path, with a girl sitting outside.

That girl was me.

For as long as I can remember, I was the girl who couldn't walk—the one who stayed home. Mama would hike to the fields or the market. "Stay close to the house," she would warn before she left, as her eyes skittered nervously down the hill and into the pori—the bush.

I always intended to do exactly as Mama instructed. But I was seven, and it was hard to stay home. I wanted to hike to the fields with Mama or to fetch water like the other girls in our village. But my legs were too thin and too weak. So instead, I sat outside our house on a thatch mat, waiting for Mama to come home.

One day, I was sitting outside, when a splash interrupted my thoughts. Girls were playing at the small spring by the side of our house. I couldn't see them, but I could hear their laughter spilling like water from the rocks.

It was hot outside. My legs were itchy, and I was tired of sitting on that mat by myself. Soon the sun grew so hot, and the splashing grew so loud that Mama's warning fell out of my head. I started to think of a thousand reasons why I needed to go to the spring. *I can fetch water. I can wash clothes. Mama will be thrilled with my helpful idea.*

I knew I could do it. The spring was close to our house, and even though I couldn't walk, I was good at crawling on my hands and knees. Only one question remained. How would I carry the water?

An idea came to me. In our cooking hut, I found a string and a small plastic jug. I tied the string to the jug and crawled forward, proudly pulling the jug behind me like a goat on the way to the market. *I can fetch water like everyone else*, I congratulated myself.

When I arrived at the spring, the other girls were standing in a shallow pool of water—jugs, upside down, above their own heads. The water looked cool and refreshing. In that moment I forgot all my plans to wash clothes.

"Friends, someone pour water on me!" I cried in excitement. Gasirimu turned to look at me. She lived a few houses away. We were the same age, born in the same week. Mama called her my twin. "Pour water on me!" I repeated. Gasirimu lifted her jug, and the shock of cold rushed down my back. I screamed, and we collapsed in laughter.

It wasn't until I was very wet that I remembered my plan to fetch water and wash clothes for Mama. *There's still time. I'll move quickly;* I told myself. Gasirimu filled my jug. I twisted the cover. Then I grabbed the string and started to crawl back toward the house, pulling the jug behind me. Suddenly, the string stretched taut and snapped out of my hand. I glared behind me. The jug, swollen with water, hadn't budged. It was too heavy for me to pull.

Why can't I fetch water like everyone else? I thought in exasperation. But then I remembered Gasirimu. She could help. The path to our house was nothing for her, ten steps away. Gasirimu agreed. She quickly ran up the slope, set the jug by our door, and sprinted away.

I started climbing, but it was not so easy for me. My wet clothes rubbed at my skin and dragged in the dirt. The sun didn't feel so hot anymore. My legs were starting to shake with cold.

As I reached the kifagio plants at the edge of our yard, a shadow fell on the dirt. I looked up. It was Mama. She was standing in front of me, her face slick with sweat, firewood balanced on her head. My younger brother, Tera, was standing next to her with his own small bundle of sticks in his arms. I looked down at my own empty hands.

"Argentine, where did you go?" Mama asked slowly.

I opened my mouth, but no words came out.

"Did you go down to the spring?" she asked.

"No, Mama," I answered quickly this time. I widened my eyes and scooted my body closer to the cooking hut, where I should have stayed.

As I leaned forward, I was discouraged to find my shirt clinging suspiciously to my body. I pinched the wet fabric away from my skin hoping Mama wouldn't notice.

"Are you sure you didn't go down to the water?" Mama asked again.

If only my legs would stop shaking, I thought. But then I realized that Mama wasn't looking at my legs. She wasn't even looking at my wet shirt. She was staring at the ground behind me.

My heart left my stomach. Maybe there was a spider, or a snake, or a line of army ants. When you crawl on the ground, there are so many dangers hidden in the dirt.

I spun frantically toward the ground behind me then sighed in relief. There were no insects or snakes. There was only a long, dark line etched into the earth.

Where did that come from? I wondered. Then I realized it was me—my own dripping body. I had left a trail in the dirt—showing exactly where I had been.

"Argentine, it's not safe for you..." Mama said, as she glanced down the hill and into the pori, where the bushes grew wild and thick. But the pori was far away, and I wasn't listening. I was still looking regretfully at my trail on the ground—the one Mama had seen.

Gasirimu hadn't left a single footstep in the dirt.

If only I could walk, I thought in frustration, *Mama never would have caught me.*

Chapter 2

I didn't understand at the time, but my mother was facing an impossible task—trying to keep us all safe in the hills of Masisi. She had three young children and a husband who was often gone. We needed sweet potatoes and cassava from the fields. We needed wood for the fire and salt from the market. Mama couldn't stay home, and she couldn't carry three children with her.

Soon, she came up with a new plan. She started leaving my younger brothers home with me. "This way you won't be alone," she explained as she left for the fields.

I was happy to have my brothers with me. They were my legs. I'd send them to fetch sticks for the fire or water for the beans, and they'd run happily in the direction I sent them.

Until one day I called my brothers, and they didn't come.

I had been sitting outside our cooking hut waiting for the beans to soften. The birds were chirping in the avocado tree, and I was convinced that if I sat quietly enough, one of the birds would land on the ground nearby. I'd topple forward and snare the bird in my hands, and we'd roast it for dinner that night.

I had been sitting there dreaming of roasted bird when a bitter smell hit my nose. The beans were burning. I needed more water.

"Tera! Espoir! Fetch some water!" I called. No response. "Come quickly!" I shouted again. Still no answer. "Terrraaaaa! Espoir!" I called one more time, but it was no use. My brothers were gone, and I was alone.

I wasn't worried about my brothers. I knew where they were. Our cousins lived nearby, and my brothers were always running down the path to play. They would be fine. *But what about me? What about our beans?* I knew my brothers never should have left me alone.

Wait till they return. I'll teach them a lesson, I thought. My mother was always so soft on my brothers. At night, if they peed in their sleep, Mama would talk to them gently. Then she would wake them early in the morning when the air was cold, and the ground was wet. "Run outside and drink the dew off the mahole leaves," she would tell them. And they would run through the shrubs and under the banana stalks with the cold, wet earth shocking their feet. When they reached the mahole leaves, they would squat low, crane their necks, and tilt the wide leaves into their mouths. Parents in our village told children that the dew from mahole leaves would solve nighttime problems. It was a punishment disguised as a cure. No one wanted to wake early and run barefoot on the cold, wet ground.

I was not interested in disguising any punishments. I slept on a mat between my brothers at night, and I thought their punishments should have been more direct. "Let me teach them a lesson," I'd beg, and my mother would click her tongue and wave me off gently.

But now Mama wasn't home, and this was my chance to teach my brothers a lesson. I waited anxiously for them to return. Tera was a quiet child, with a long face like my grandfather's. But Espoir bubbled with energy. He was always leading Tera off in different directions.

By the time my brothers returned, the beans had soaked up all their water and I had marinated in my frustration. "Tera! Espoir! Come here!" I demanded as soon as I saw them. They hovered nearby, standing an arm's length away. "Ngwino!" I called them closer, but they shuffled their feet and stayed in one place.

Finally, tired of waiting, I snapped forward and grabbed for Tera's wrist. He jumped back. If only I could stand and chase him. But I was stuck on the ground, and Tera was like one of those birds in the avocado tree. I could only dream of catching him. I could see it already—a lifetime spent with my brothers running away and me sitting on the ground with my skinny legs by my side.

Espoir grinned. His bare feet were jumping with laughter. Even Tera was smiling. That's when it occurred to me. My brothers were young. They'd make the same mistake again. I was a girl, older and wiser, and next time I would be ready.

The next day that Tera and Espoir snuck off to play, I sat outside the cooking hut preparing myself. I arranged my face into a blank expression, the way Mama arranged her face when I asked too many questions.

After a while, Tera and Espoir returned home. This time, I pretended not to notice them. I sang a song to myself. At first, they looked at me warily and circled wide in the dirt, careful not to step within arm's reach. I waited. The beans boiled in the pot, and the flat lid danced, but my face gave away nothing. Soon my brothers began to forget their own misdeeds. Their circles around me grew narrower. Their memories grew shorter. I sat on my mat waiting for my prey. Tera made the first mistake. He got lost in his games and galloped carelessly past me.

Pah! I lunged at his ankles, throwing my whole body at him. I was smaller than Tera, but an unexpected attack from the ground can topple anyone. Tera fell, and I pressed myself on top of him, pinning him with my arms.

"Ehe, let's see you run from me now!" I exclaimed, victorious. I might not be able to catch a bird, but I could snare my brother. Tera wriggled beneath me, but he couldn't escape. He was stuck like a tongue between teeth. I pulled my shoulders back and unclenched my fists—exhausted and satisfied. I had won that battle.

It wasn't until later that night that my worries returned. My brothers and I were lying on our mats while the smoke from Mama's cooking fire slipped through our roof. I always slept between my brothers at night. The heat from their bodies kept my thin legs warm. My thoughts returned to the events of the day: Tera and Espoir running down the path and me sitting outside our house alone. I'd never be able to keep up with my brothers. I'd always be the one left behind.

In that moment, I knew the truth. I needed my brothers—I needed everyone—more than they needed me.

Lying on my mat that night, I still didn't know what dangers were waiting outside, but I had seen Mama's worried expression every time that she left for the fields—the way her eyes slid down the hill and into the pori. Whatever danger was waiting out there, I didn't want to face it alone.

"Tera, Espoir," I whispered into the darkness, trying to sweeten my voice. "Have mercy on me. Don't ever leave me alone."

Chapter 3

My brothers were boys—eager to run—and no matter how I sweetened my voice, I knew they wouldn't stay home with me every day. So, I started inviting other girls to come to our house. We'd sit in a circle and throw an avocado seed into the air, seeing how many rocks we could pick up before the seed came back. It was like a game of jacks. One, two, three, four...up to twelve rocks I'd pick up at a time. I loved that game, and I loved having those girls nearby, but they couldn't stay forever, and soon I would find myself home alone again.

Sometimes I crawled down the dirt path to visit Uncle Manassé and Aunt Kampire. They lived a few houses away, close enough for me to crawl on my own. The yard outside their house was filled with pebbles that bit into my skin, but I still loved visiting their house.

Uncle Manassé was light-skinned and tall, with scars on his face. Whenever he saw me, he'd lean down and reach out to me, whispering, "Take this banana, hide it somewhere, and soon it will sweeten."

Aunt Kampire was generous too. She knew how to make everyone feel welcome. "Argentine, have you come to visit us today?" she would ask, whenever I crawled through the door, as though I was an honored visitor. She always had something for me to do. At her house, I felt like a person of meaning. "Have you come to pluck the cassava leaves?" she'd ask, and I'd nod happily.

When I finished plucking the leaves, I'd play with my cousin, Sifa, the only girl in their family. We'd fashion dolls out of deep purple banana buds, bathe them in water, and tie them onto our backs.

But soon the days of making dolls and tossing avocado seeds came to an end. The other girls stopped having time to play. Even Sifa had learned to pound cassava. One day, I arrived at Aunt Kampire's house and found Sifa towering over a wooden mortar. Sifa was younger than me, but that mortar was as tall as me. My hope sank. How was I ever going to pound cassava like Sifa?

Another day I saw Gasirimu walking back from our spring, long-legged and lanky. She was balancing a large yellow jug of water on her head. I saw Gasirimu often, but this time it was different. Her legs were longer, and the jug was bigger. *Gasirimu carries water for her mother,* I thought. I looked at my thin legs tucked by my side. All at once, my eyes opened. I saw Gasirimu, and I saw myself.

That night, I sat inside by the cooking fire as Mama stirred tomatoes and onions into a sauce. The oil sizzled and popped. Our wooden door was already shut for the night, but my mind was trapped outside on the dirt path where I'd seen Gasirimu walking like a woman. "Mama, tell me," I began. "Is Gasirimu really my age?"

"You're twins. You were born the same week in the same year," my mother answered. My future disappeared before me that day, like a mist covering the road ahead. In a world where everyone walked, who could I be?

In hopes of finding an answer to that question, I started watching the other children in our village more carefully. One morning I noticed that they were all gone. There were no girls fetching water at the spring or sweeping the dirt outside their houses. There were no boys running down the path.

"Where have all the other children gone?" I asked my mother.

"They're at school," she answered.

I looked up at Mama. *Why didn't anyone tell me about school?* Questions spilled from my mouth. "Where is this school? What's it like there? What do they learn?"

The more Mama told me about school, the more I wanted to go. My brothers were too young, but I was sure that I was ready. At night, I lay on my thatch mat, imagining how I might convince Mama to let me go to school. In our village, they said that a child is old enough to start school when she can reach her arm over the top of her head and touch her ear. I crossed my arm over my head and wiggled my fingers until I found my ear.

"Mama, look at this!" I squealed with my arm twisted around my head. "I'm ready for school!"

"Oh yes, you've grown up," Mama drew out her words. "But the school is far away. How will you get there?"

I untwisted my arm and pulled my shoulders straight. "I'll carry myself," I said in a whoosh. I was already picturing myself at this place called school. It couldn't be that far away, and I was good at crawling. I could even crawl on my elbows.

Mama didn't look so convinced, but I was good at talking until everyone else grew silent, and eventually Mama agreed to talk to my father. I don't know what she said to him or where she found the money, but a few days later, Mama said she would register me at the school.

The following morning, before the dew had dried on the mahole leaves, Mama announced it was time for us to walk to school to register me. I was ready. The day before, I had found

11

my brothers' old broken flip-flops, and now I was tying the foam onto my knees. When Mama saw me, she hesitated, and I thought that she would refuse. "Stay close to the house," she would say, like she always did.

But she didn't say anything. She looked at the foam on my knees and led me onto the dirt path.

At first, it was easy. The path was flat. But soon I grew tired. My wrists burned hot, and my hands felt heavy, as though I could no longer lift them. My elbows refused to straighten. As I crawled forward, all I could see was the dirt path, stretching endlessly in front of me.

Earlier, there had been other children walking nearby. I recognized them from church, and a few had greeted me politely as their legs swooshed by my head. But their shapes had faded into the distance, and the footpath had grown empty and long.

When I was too tired to continue, Mama stopped. She pointed at a light glinting in the distance. Under the bright light I saw two long rectangular shapes—wooden school buildings covered with shiny metal roofs reflecting the sun. I was accustomed to houses built from the earth, with mud walls and thatched roofs. These were different. They were the largest, most beautiful buildings I had ever seen. There were so many doors. Students were playing outside. Their hands beat out the rhythm of a song. *This is the place. This is where all the children go*, I rejoiced. *There will be a place for me here.*

The only problem was that my mother and I were perched on a precipice. A cliff lay before us. Carved into the side of the hill were rough steps, ledges of dirt. In order to reach the school, we had to climb down.

I started to move, lowering myself step by step. My shoulders burned as I braced on each ledge. Finally, we reached one of the long wooden buildings, and Mama led me through one of the doors.

"I want to enroll my child in school," she said to a tall man with polished shoes and creased pants.

"Ah...yes...yes. She must start school," the man said. He bent forward and inspected me through his glasses, "Only...how far away do you live? How will she get here every day?"

My heart thundered, but Mama looked calm.

"My daughter says that she will carry herself," she answered.

"No! No!" The man with glasses flew to a standing position, leaving me behind with his polished shoes. "That will not be possible. A child like this..." He rubbed at the back of his neck, looking for words. "She cannot carry herself."

I dropped my head to the ground and started to turn back to the door, but Mama didn't move. There was a long silence. I wondered if she was twirling her tongue in her mouth. That's what she told me to do when I was talking too much. "Before you take a word out of your mouth, circle your tongue seven times," she would say.

Finally, Mama spoke. "Have mercy on us," she said to the man with polished shoes. Her voice was soft, and her head was lowered, but I was sitting on the ground, looking at her feet. They were planted, strong and firm, like a tree. Mama stood there while the man started and stumbled and started again.

"I suppose she can try..." he said at last.

That day, as we returned to the house, I was so happy that I barely noticed the climb up the cliff or the long dirt path leading me home. My future had arrived, and I was ready for it.

Chapter 4

The next day, I woke with the first morning light. I was ready to start school. It was still cold in the house, and usually I stayed under my blanket in the morning until Mama returned from her prayers. When she returned, she'd send my brothers to borrow sparks of fire from our neighbor's house. The smell of burning leaves would fill the house, and the cold air would depart. Only then, would I crawl out from under my blanket.

But on this day, even the cold couldn't stop me. I was excited to start school, and I was ready to carry myself. I knew Mama couldn't walk with me to school every day for the same reason she couldn't stay home with us every day. She needed to fetch firewood and harvest crops from the field.

That morning, I prepared to crawl to school on my own. I couldn't carry a bag because I needed my hands for crawling. Mama placed a new notebook and Bic pen in a plastic bag. Then she pinned the bag to my shirt.

I crawled eagerly onto the path. "God protect you," Mama called out. She must have been scared. For all my life, Mama had been telling me to stay close—close to the house, close to the fire, close to my brothers. Now, I was crawling far away.

By the time I arrived at school that first day, the sun was hot, and the other students were already standing in lines. I stopped at the edge of the group and stared at the lines of students. There were so many shoes—so many feet. They shuffled and stomped in the dirt. I would be crushed.

One of the teachers saw me. She had mercy on me and waved me into the classroom ahead of the others. I crawled through the door and lifted myself onto one of the low wooden benches. Soon, crowds of sweaty students pushed in behind me. A teacher, with his shirt tucked in and his pants pressed smart, rapped on the table, and the class fell silent. The teacher called attendance. When it was my turn, I called out "present," and snapped my finger into the air with a sharp clicking sound. The other students turned to look at me and started to whisper.

A few students hurried into the classroom late. The teacher sent them outside to weed. And then there were students who faced the worst fate of all—being sent home. "Your parents haven't paid for a month," the director boomed before they even reached the classroom.

Next, it was time for the lesson. The teacher was speaking in French, and I couldn't understand his words, but the other students were opening notebooks and taking out pens, so I reached into my plastic bag and took out my notebook. It smelled fresh as I folded back the soft blue cover and exposed the first page, smoothing it gently. The teacher turned to the chalkboard, and I picked up my pen, ready to copy whatever he wrote. I was going to learn to write.

The teacher drew shapes on the board, and I copied each one. Suddenly, I stopped and glowered at my notebook. There was a brown spot on the fresh white page. I tried to brush it off, but it only grew. I tilted my head and checked the other students sitting nearby. Their pages gleamed white. I looked back at my notebook, and it seemed even dirtier. *What is wrong with my notebook?* I asked myself. *Maybe Espoir got it dirty.*

15

I flipped to the next page and creased it gently. I was falling behind. As the teacher finished writing, I picked up my pen and began copying the shapes again, but then I stopped. This page was dirty too. I shook my head in disbelief. *What terrible luck!*

At midday, a whistle pierced the air. My classmates jumped to their feet and skipped out of the building. I sat motionless on the low wooden bench, wishing I could join the tumbling crowd. But I knew I'd only be trampled or laughed at. I didn't want anyone to see me hoisting myself up the steps with my arms. I didn't want them to see my fingernails digging into the dirt and my legs bent beneath me. So even though I was hungry, I waited in that classroom until everyone else left. When the air settled into silence, I crawled out of the building and up the dirt stairs carved into the slope. Then I started my long journey home.

It was late in the day when I arrived at our house. I knew the other students had arrived hours earlier. But still, I was proud. I had gone to school like everyone else.

When I arrived, Tera and Espoir were outside with my mother. "Did you get tired today?" Mama asked.

"Yes, I was tired," I agreed, thinking of the long path to school, and the feet ready to trample me, and the notebook with pages that wouldn't stay white. *What's wrong with my notebook*, I wondered again. I tilted my head toward Mama and started to ask that question, but then I noticed how tired Mama's face looked. Her skin was dripping with sweat, and her eyes were red from blowing on flames. Every two days, Mama hiked into the hills looking for firewood. And with every fire, Mama would lean close to the sparks and blow until tears ran down her cheeks from the bitter grey smoke.

I cleared my throat and softened my words. "I was tired...but only a little."

Mama didn't need to know how exhausted I was. And she didn't need to know about my dirty notebook. There was only one thing Mama needed to know. "School was good," I answered, beaming at Mama. "I am going to be just like everyone else."

Chapter 5

The path to school seemed to grow longer every day, and I arrived later and later. I'd slip into the classroom and climb on a bench, hoping the teacher wouldn't send me out to weed with the other latecomers.

On my slow journey home in the afternoons, I began to look around more. I noticed the older boys gathered by the sides of the path, joking and playing. Some of them had chukudus—scooters made from branches tied together and wheels cut from the cross section of trees. The chukudus had no motors or brakes. They were handmade scooters that probably seemed small to everyone else. To me, they were large and fast-moving.

At first, the rolling chukudus scared me. I would scramble to the side of the path and tuck in my fingers as the boys on their chukudus careened carelessly past me. But as I watched the boys, I started to think about how much easier it would be to ride on a chukudu and how much sooner I could arrive home if only those boys would push me. I'd heard Mama say to my father at night, "If only we had money to pay someone to push Argentine on a chukudu."

"There's no money for that," my father had answered.

Gathering my courage, I called out to the boys one afternoon. "Can't you push me on your chukudu?" I asked, sweetening my voice. The boys with the chukudu laughed. They were surprised by my request. But one of them agreed.

"Just for a little while," he shrugged. As I climbed on the wooden frame of the scooter and crossed my legs in front of the steering pole, I was already beginning to regret my idea. The boy started to push. The footpath was bumpier than I had imagined. My weak legs flew in the air. I held onto the steering pole with one hand and gathered my legs with the other hand. We were starting to pick up speed.

"Waa! Look at her!" other students called as I rolled past. No one understood how hard it was for me to hang on. Finally, the chukudu wobbled to a stop. The boy peered at me curiously as I climbed off the chukudu.

"We've really helped you today," he said, proud of himself and unaware of how terrified I'd been. I smiled back. Now that we had stopped, I was grateful for the ride on the chukudu, even if it had scared me. If only we could have paid that boy to push me slowly and carefully every day.

But we couldn't. So instead, I crawled home each day, hoping to stumble on a free ride. If I found a group of boys, I'd take my chance and ask them to push me again. Sometimes they helped me generously, pushing me far down the path. But other times they went too fast. One time, I climbed on a chukudu, and several boys leaned to push. They hooted and hollered, and I bounced precariously as I clutched my legs with one hand and the steering pole with the other until my fingers could hold on no longer. I fell off the chukudu and tumbled hard to the ground. A rock cut into my shoulder. By the time I opened my eyes, I was sprawled on the empty dirt path, alone again. The boys had scattered, afraid of getting in trouble. There was nothing left for me to do but pick myself up and continue crawling home.

That evening, I showed my mother the cut on my shoulder. She cleaned it off gently and wrapped her arms around me.

Suddenly, I remembered my notebook, with pages that still wouldn't stay white, and a question fell off my tongue before I could bite it back.

"Tell me! What is wrong with my notebook?" I begged. "Why won't it stay clean?"

Mama flinched and sucked in her breath as she lifted my hands and traced the dirt around my fingers. *Ehh! My hands!* I was making my own notebook dirty. I rubbed my fingers furiously. When the dirt started to fade, I breathed in relief. There was no water at school, but I could rub that dirt off my hands.

I was still confident that nothing could stop me from going to school. That was before I met the cows.

Chapter 6

In the afternoons, in the hills of Masisi, cowherds drive their cows home from the pastures. It isn't one cow; it is herds of terrible beasts. The first time I encountered them, I was crawling home from school. Suddenly the ground started to vibrate, and I saw a herd of cows with long, sharp horns, thudding down the path in front of me. They bellowed and grunted. Each cow was enormous—ten times my size. And there I was—a tiny speck on the footpath with nowhere to go. I'd be crushed. Mama would never even find my bones.

I spun my head, looking for a place to hide. On one side of the path was a sharp hill, too steep for me to scramble up. On the other side was a ditch with some shrubs. The cows lumbered closer. I couldn't even see the cowherd. He was too far behind, but I could hear his stick smacking their hides. He was driving the cows down the path and straight into me. It was just like I'd always feared. I was alone, and there was no one to save me.

Without another thought, I threw myself off the path. I rolled into the ditch and scrambled under a bush, squeezing my eyes shut. Above me, the cows stopped to chomp on grass. I didn't dare make a sound, not even to cough.

I stayed under the bush for a long time—until I could hear nothing, not even the sound of the cowherd's airy whistle and the thwack of his stick. Only then did my heart return to my stomach. I climbed back onto the path to continue my journey home.

The next day I didn't go to school. I was so terrified of the cows that I couldn't even leave the house. I knew I was too small to face those cows alone.

Finally, an idea came to me. The other people on the path could help me. I woke up early the next day and carried myself back to school. I arrived at the school as the other students sang "Debout Congolais," the national anthem. In the classroom, I wiped my hands clean. Then, I opened my notebook and copied the letters the teacher wrote on the blackboard. I was no longer worried about my notebook growing dirty. I was thinking of only one thing—the journey home.

When the whistle sounded at the end of the school day, I climbed slowly up the dirt steps and onto the path. I tilted my head and listened for cows. It was quiet. I started to move forward. As soon as I saw people coming down the footpath, I broke out in a grin and greeted them enthusiastically. "Hello. Good afternoon," I called from the ground. "By the way, did you see any cows on the path?"

Sometimes, people reported that they had seen cows. On those days, I continued carefully down the path, one ear tilted up, listening for the first bellow, prepared to throw myself off the path before I even saw the cows.

On other days, people told me they hadn't seen any cows, and I carried myself a little more confidently. But some days, there were no people to ask. Those were the worst days. Sometimes the cows would arrive without warning, and I would throw myself violently off the path. On those days, when I arrived home, I would report breathlessly back to my mother, "The cows, they almost killed me today!"

"My child, cows don't want to hurt people," Mama would say softly, trying to comfort me. But even if Mama was right, I wasn't convinced that a cow would recognize me as a person. I'd spent a long time thinking about it. Everyone else walked on two feet. I crawled on the ground. To a cow, I did not look like a person.

Determined to avoid a confrontation with the cows, I continued asking questions of everyone I knew. "Tell me," I said to Aunt Kampire one day as I plucked cassava leaves outside her house, "Do cows eat people sometimes?"

"Oh no!" she chuckled. "Cows never eat people." She pointed off toward a hill where cows were grazing. There was a mother cow with her calf suckling underneath. The calf was small and tucked under its mother. *Maybe these cows aren't so dangerous,* I thought in relief.

But Aunt Kampire continued, "Of course, you must be careful of those horns. They like to fight each other."

My heart began to thud again. I had known the truth. From the first day I saw those horns and those hooves, I understood their danger. It didn't matter whether a cow wanted to hurt me or not. I knew my size, and I knew theirs. In a world filled with cows, I'd never be safe.

Chapter 7

While I was trying to escape the cows, other problems arose. My parents had no more money for school fees. For a while, the director with the shiny shoes had mercy on me. Long after another student would have been sent home, the director let me slip into class. But one day, I arrived at school, exhausted from my journey, and the director called out my name before I could reach the classroom door.

"Argentine, you have to go home," he said sadly. "Tell your father he has to pay something." I slumped forward. I already knew my father's answer to that.

I'll never forget my journey home that day. The path was so quiet. There were no other students—no other people at all. It was the wrong time of day. Everyone had already arrived wherever they were going. It was only me, alone on an empty path, carrying myself back to where I had started.

After that day, I stopped going to school. I returned home and tried to forget about the long buildings with the children singing and clapping outside.

But there was one question that wouldn't leave my mind. Why were there no other children like me? I had seen so many children at that school. There were rows and rows of children. Tall and short. Boys and girls. But there were no other children like me. In our village, I'd never seen anyone like me.

There was only one place where I found people like me, and that was at church. Every Sunday, Mama would comb her hair into a circle, rub oil on our skin, and lead us to church. I would sit on a wooden bench, listening carefully, as the pastor talked about the Bible. In the Bible, there were people like me. There was a man who couldn't walk, and a man who couldn't hear, and a woman who couldn't stop bleeding.

At home, I wanted to learn more about the people in the Bible—the ones like me. On a sunny day, I followed Mama outside. "Did Jesus really heal the man who couldn't hear?" I asked.

Mama looked up from pounding cassava root. "Oh yes, God be praised," she answered, distractedly.

"And what about the man who couldn't walk?" I continued.

"Jesus healed him too," Mama agreed easily. She was so busy pounding her stick into the mortar that she didn't see me wrapping foam around my knees, getting ready to crawl down the footpath.

"So where is Jesus? Where can I find this man who will heal me?" I asked.

When Mama looked up, she glanced at the foam on my knees and the eager expression on my face. Then she tilted her head to the sky. After a while, she spoke.

"One day, God willing, we'll go to the Centre Pour Handi-capés in Goma. There are girls like you there," she said gently.

But I didn't want to hear about the Centre Pour Handicapés in the city of Goma. It sounded far away, and I was sure that this man called Jesus was right nearby. He could heal me. I just needed to find him. I was like Zacchaeus, looking for Jesus in a crowd. I only needed to climb a tree, and I was sure I would see Jesus.

"But where is Jesus?" I pressed my mother again. Finally, she answered.

25

"He's...he's not here anymore. He doesn't walk on this earth. He's in heaven now," she admitted.

My thoughts jerked to a stop. Heaven sounded even further away than the city of Goma. "What do you mean he is not here?" I cried, thinking of all the times the pastor talked about Jesus.

For months, I couldn't stop thinking about this question. I had to find Jesus. Who would know more about Jesus than Mama? The answer came to me like a tree came to Zacchaeus. My grandfather. He would know where to find Jesus. Grandfather was a pastor, and Mama always said that he taught her everything she knew about God.

The next morning, I followed Mama outside into the cold air. "Mama, let's visit my grandfather," I proposed.

Mama looked up, an avocado in her hand. "Oh. Your grandfather? He loves you, but he is far away," she answered vaguely.

"So, what day will we go?" I continued.

"It's too far. Don't you remember going to school? It's much farther than that," Mama insisted.

I nodded again, but there was no stopping me. Every day, I pestered Mama. "When are you taking me to see my grandfather?" Mama would shake her head and tell me to circle my tongue seven times.

One day, she answered me. "Shall I call you Gasuku?"

I sat there in silence, wondering who Gasuku was—trying to think of a person in the Bible named Gasuku. Maybe I hadn't listened to the Bible stories well enough. It was only later that I learned that gasuku meant parrot.

Even if Mama called me a parrot, I was not giving up. I was like the woman who bled for ten years. I knew that if only I could touch Jesus's robe, I would be healed.

"When will we visit my grandfather?" I kept asking until one day Mama gave in.

"We'll go tomorrow," she answered.

I was thrilled, but Mama immediately tried to tamp down my excitement. "It's a long way. We might not make it," she warned.

"God will help us," I answered confidently. Mama couldn't argue with that.

Chapter 8

We woke early the next day and started our journey, leaving Espoir and Tera behind with my father. "I have to return soon for your brothers," Mama warned, but I wasn't thinking about my brothers. I was excited to go.

We passed rows of banana plants and mounds of beans. When I grew tired, Mama carried me. All day, we traveled until the big orange sun started to dip behind the hills.

As evening came, Mama grew nervous. She started scanning the hills like she did back in Shahalia. Finally, she pointed at a muddy brown break in the green—a cluster of houses on the hill ahead. "That is Shangazi's house. We'll stop there for the night," she explained. At Shangazi's house we drank water, ate ugali, and slept on mats on the floor.

The next morning, we started climbing again. This time, the path turned down a long, steep hill. Down and down we climbed, until I could no longer imagine any return. There was only forward—only the next step. When we arrived at the bottom of the hill, I stopped and stared. In front of us were fields of bright green grass, sturdy houses with yellow and pink flowers in front, and dirt yards swept neat and clean. It was beautiful.

"Look at that building with the tin roof. That's the church," Mama said. "Your grandfather's house is behind there."

We started moving again. As we made our way toward the house, people began to recognize Mama. "You've returned home," a woman said, and I wondered for the first time why

Mama had left such a beautiful place. Even the mud houses were better here. They glowed in a warm orange color and a swirling design.

"This is it," Mama said, stopping in front of a large house where a stout woman was washing dishes in a plastic basin outside. Mama dropped her voice to a whisper, "That's your grandfather's wife."

The woman stopped her washing and looked at us in surprise. "Have you come all the way here?" the woman asked. She stood and ushered us into the house.

From the moment we entered my grandfather's house, I knew it was a place I never wanted to leave. The floor was swept. The living room was filled with wooden benches and chairs. It was a house made for visitors.

I was still smiling at all the benches when my grandfather walked into the room. He was the finest man I had ever seen, with grey hair and two rows of straight, white teeth. He squatted low and hugged me.

Soon, my mother left to return to my brothers, but I stayed for weeks at my grandfather's house. I loved it there. There were so many visitors, and my grandfather presented me proudly to every visitor. We ate potatoes cooked in palm oil and shining orange. We drank tea that was milky and sweet. My grandfather had a two-burner kerosene stove in his living room and, whenever a visitor arrived, my grandfather would put the kettle on to boil.

The first time I saw my grandfather light a match and turn the knob on his stovetop, I was stunned by the magic of the flame that leapt at his command. I thought of Mama squatting to light fires with sparks she borrowed from neighbors and leaves that hissed and spat smoke into her eyes. I wondered again why my mother had ever left this wonderful place.

At my grandfather's house, I felt safe. No one drank banana beer, and no one argued. The food never lacked salt or oil. And, every evening, my grandfather would light a kerosene lamp and lead us through the night air into the church to sing and pray. There was one song that stuck in my heart:

I come before you as a small child

I need your help very much

In all things in life

In the times I am tested in this world

Strengthen me, my King

On this journey I am on, may I not go alone

In that church lit by a lamp, I sang those words like my own prayer. "May I not go alone. May I not go alone." That was my song.

Chapter 9

I loved my grandfather's house, but I also missed my mother. I'd never been away from her for so many days. I couldn't stop thinking about her, back at our house in Shahalia, fetching firewood and lighting fires. It was time to go home.

When I returned to Shahalia, I joined the children's choir at our church, anxious to sing just like I'd sung at my grandfather's church. The choir leader was a boy named Safari. He had a smiling face and warts on his feet. I was too close to the ground, and I always noticed other people's feet. I pushed my gaze up and tried to concentrate on Safari's face.

"Whoever learns this song the best will get a prize next week," he said.

That caught my attention. *I can learn a song*, I thought. It didn't matter if Safari taught the song in Swahili, Kinyarwanda, French, or any other language. I was going to learn that song better than anyone else. I had more time than all the other children. While they were busy going to school or carrying water or planting sorghum, I was at home practicing that song.

The next week when we returned to rehearsal, I won the prize—red and yellow pieces of candy, but it wasn't the candy that thrilled me. It was the sense of belonging. In choir, my voice was like everyone else's voice. They might be the children who went to school. They might be the children who stood up straight. But when we opened our mouths to sing, our voices came out together. I loved that feeling.

I became friends with a girl named Bébé. She was Safari's sister. Her mother had died, and her father had remarried. I knew that Bébé's life was difficult. Sometimes at night, I could hear Bébé's father erupting angrily at her. I'd open our door and wait for Bébé to come running. Then we'd lie under my blanket together. "Someday life will be different," I'd say to Bébé.

One evening, Bébé asked why I didn't go with the children's choir on Saturdays.

"Go with you where?" I responded.

Bébé's face lit with excitement, as she told me how they traveled to churches in the area, walking for hours over winding paths to reach a village on a hill far away. When they arrived, the youth choir would sleep in the church at night and sing the next day.

"It's too far for me," I said sadly. I couldn't even crawl to school. I'd only been able to visit my grandfather because my mother had come with me. I'd never be able to crawl to another village.

I thought that was the end of the discussion, but one Saturday morning, Bébé and the other choir girls came to our house. "We need Argentine to come with us," Bébé announced to my mother.

"It is too far for Argentine," Mama answered gently. No one wanted to hurt Bébé's feelings. She'd already been hurt enough.

"I'll carry her," Bébé insisted, offering a smile that Mama couldn't refuse.

"I will, too," one of the other girls, named Magambo, chimed in. Mama's eyes widened. Magambo was the pastor's daughter—a girl so shy that she barely spoke a word. Now, even Magambo was asking for Mama's permission.

"Why do you want Argentine to go?" Mama asked cautiously.

"We need her voice," Bébé insisted, smiling one more time. Finally, Mama agreed.

I could see from Mama's face that she was nervous. But I was thrilled that someone had finally needed me, and I didn't want to disappoint them.

All day those girls carried me, one after another, until we arrived at a village I had never seen before. I wasn't nervous until we gathered to eat. The congregation offered us ugali. I forced a smile onto my face and pretended to eat with my friends, pinching off tiny portions of ugali and dipping them slowly in the cassava leaf sauce. I raised a cup to my mouth and let the water touch my lips but didn't dare swallow. A terrible question had appeared in my mind. I didn't know where the latrine was. I only knew it would be far away, up a steep path—somewhere I couldn't reach on my own. I was filled with embarrassment. Who would carry me to the latrine? What if I fell in? That night I regretted my journey.

But the following day, when the sun rose, I forgot all my hunger and shame when the pastor called us to the front of the church. My friends stood in rows, and I sat beside them on the dirt floor where the congregation could hardly see me. We started our song. I sang the verse, and the choir repeated the chorus back to me, like we'd practiced.

As I sang, the women in the church started to murmur. They craned their necks and rose to their feet. "Where is the girl who is singing?" I heard an old woman ask. Then she saw me sitting on the ground with my legs curled beside me. The old woman clasped her hands together. "God is full of amazements," I heard her declare. "Look at that girl! She sings just like the rest!"

Chapter 10

After our choir returned to Shahalia, we received wonderful news. Visitors were coming all the way from the city of Goma. There was no greater honor than the arrival of visitors in our hills. The whole village was swept up in excitement. Men started fixing church walls and building new latrines. Women weeded the grounds of the church and swept the yard clean. My father built the second floor of our house, where the honorable visitors could stay. Mama began stacking young bananas and avocados that would ripen on the day our guests arrived. A goat would be slaughtered. Pots of green bananas would be cooked. My father and Safari, the choir director, would walk all the way to the town of Mweso to meet our visitors and lead them back to our village.

When the day arrived, my father left our house wearing a jacket and tie, his pants creased sharp with an iron. I rushed to the kifagio plants at the side of our house, fashioned a short broom out of the leaves, and swept our front yard, scooting along the dirt, clearing every stick, like Mama had taught me. I liked sweeping. It was a sign that we were expecting visitors, and there was nothing I loved more than visitors.

I peppered my mother with questions. "What will the visitors look like? How much longer before they arrive?" Mama reminded me to circle my tongue, but I could barely contain my excitement.

The next day, my father returned with the visitors. I stared up at them eagerly. Their jackets and pants were wrinkled, and their shoes were covered with dark mud. *It must be a very long way to Mweso,* I thought, looking at the strange color of the mud.

The women of our village served feasts to the men, and later the adults gathered in our house. My father lit a kerosene lamp, so that they could talk long into the night.

One of the visitors was named Pastor Amani. I heard him talking with my parents one night. "Why don't you bring Argentine to Goma?" he asked, his voice soft, and his bald head shining from the light of the kerosene lamp. "There is a center for people with disabilities. There are girls like Argentine there."

"We don't have any money for that," my father answered, but Pastor Amani continued, looking at Mama. "If you ever arrive in Goma, come to our church. Go to the neighborhood of Katindo and look for the placard that says Church Mahanaime."

The adults started talking about something else. But those words stuck in my heart that day, planted like an avocado seed. Mama had told me about the city of Goma before, but it had always sounded so far away. Now these visitors from Goma were sitting in our house. I could see them for myself. If they had traveled from Goma to Mweso to Shahalia, maybe I could travel that way in reverse. There was a place for me in Goma, if only I could find a way there.

Chapter 11

The nights were cold and dark in the hills of Masisi. By six o'clock in the evening, the sun would set, and the hills would turn blue, then black.

When we were young, my brothers and I waited eagerly for the nights of mbala mwezi to come. Those were the nights when the moon rose full and round. As soon as we saw the shape, my brothers would run from house to house shouting, "Mbala mwezi is coming! Mbala mwezi is coming! Where will we play?"

On those nights, the darkness disappeared, the moon lit the sky, and the teenage girls swept their yards so clean that the light of the moon bounced off the ground and made everything shine. All the children of Shahalia would run from one house to another. When they came to our house, I would join their singing. Someone would grab an empty container and beat it like a drum, and we'd gather in a circle.

Sometimes we would play hide-and-seek in the moonlight. I was good at hiding because I was so small. I could vanish into the blackness of the banana stalks near our house, and no one would ever find me, but I was too smart to go without a friend. "Come hide with me," I'd whisper to Bébé or Magambo, and we'd rustle through the dried leaves, pressing ourselves close to the stalks.

Eventually, my mother would call us inside. She would sing in a soft, playful voice, *"Mwenye haana kwabo alale mu muti."* *"He who has no home, sleep in a tree. He who has a home, may he go inside."* The gentle tune would usher us into our homes and under our blankets, each of us dreaming of mbala mwezi and thankful not to be sleeping in a tree.

Soon after our visitors came from Goma, Mama stopped letting us go outside for mbala mwezi. At first, I didn't understand why. "Stay inside," Mama warned as she scanned the hills and pressed the door shut.

I didn't know anything about what was happening around us. I only knew that Mama stopped smiling. She didn't want me to leave her side. She didn't want my brothers to run down the path, and she didn't want us to go out for mbala mwezi. Instead, she would call us inside in the evenings and block our door shut with three planks of wood. We passed the evenings sitting behind our wobbly door, listening for warning cries from our neighbors. Soon those cries started to arrive.

"Run! They're coming!" a neighbor would call, banging a wooden spoon on a metal pot like a drum.

That's when my mother became like a cat, who carries her young in her teeth.

Mama would stand in the smoky darkness of our house. "Tugende. Let's go," she would say, without explaining who was coming or why. Then she would lead my brothers and me out the door and into the banana stalks by the side of the house.

I remember feeling confused at first. It was cold, and the ground was damp, and I wanted to go back to our house. *Where's the danger? I don't see any danger*, I would think, as I glanced around the moon-filled night.

But children learn what their parents teach, and my mother was teaching us to hide.

Chapter 12

One afternoon I was sitting outside, while Mama swept our yard. I felt safe because it was daylight, and Mama was home.

Then we heard the cry.

"Yeee! They're coming!" a neighbor called, her voice ululating like a warning bell.

I felt naked in the daylight. At night we hid in the banana plants by the side of our house. But during the day, where could we hide?

Espoir and Tera reappeared. They had been playing down the dirt path, but now they were flocking toward Mama, like baby chicks who'd seen a hawk circling above. Espoir pressed himself into Mama's kikwembe. Tera's voice stumbled and shook as he pointed toward the path. "Everyone's running," he finally managed to say.

Mama arranged her face as she turned to Tera. "Oh really, who did you see?" she asked lightly, trying to keep us all calm. But it was too late. We could all see our neighbors tearing across the path, carrying pots of food in their hands and children on their backs. Everyone was running—everyone except us.

I turned to look at Mama. She always knew what to do. But now she was standing motionless, her hand pressed to her cheek. It was time to run. But how could Mama carry us all?

Eventually, Mama jerked into motion. "Argentine, ngwino," she said, "come." She pulled me onto her back and tied me with a kitenge cloth. Her skin smelled of oil and soap and smoke from the fire. Next, she grabbed Espoir and Tera, one on each hand. Then she ran.

We crossed the dirt path in front of our house and started uphill. But I was confused. There was nowhere to hide in this direction. There were no banana stalks. *Mama, where are you going?* I wanted to wail. Then I realized that Mama was headed straight for the hill called Gapfura. My heart left my stomach. No one wanted to hide on Gapfura. It was a bare hill with no bananas to eat and no water to drink and no place to hide.

When we reached the hill, Mama leaned forward and started to climb. It was steep and wet. Her bare feet slid in the mud. Anyone could see us—a woman with three children scrambling up the side of a hill in the daylight.

Mama grabbed onto a shrub, trying to pull herself up. "Put your foot here. Hold onto this rock," she kept telling Espoir, but he was too young to climb a hill like this. I knew what people would say if they saw us. "Why do you always carry that girl of yours?" they'd ask. "Why don't you leave her and worry about your other children?"

We reached the top of the hill and Mama slid me off her back. There was a dense thicket of reeds that I hadn't known about. We had a place to hide. I breathed in relief. Mama had known where we were going all along.

We sat in that thicket for a long time. The sun traveled across the sky. Tera, Espoir, and I began to forget where we were. Tera grabbed a stick from the ground and pretended to play a guitar. I started to sing. Mama glared at us both. "Be quiet," she shushed. "Someone will hear you."

That almost made me laugh. Who was going to hear us on an empty hill?

As the darkness approached, Mama stood up, ready to go home. I was relieved. Evening was coming. Mama tied her kikwembe tight on her waist and patted her hips. "I'm coming back soon. I must get food," she said.

Cold ran through my body as though it was starting to rain. Mama was leaving us.

I thought of our house down the hill—the open door, left-over beans still sitting in an aluminum pot by the fire. If only I had been able to carry those beans like our neighbors, Mama wouldn't be leaving us now.

"We don't need food. We can last until morning," I pleaded.

Mama shook her head. Her expression made me wonder how long we were going to stay on this hill called Gapfura. I turned to ask, but Mama had already moved away. She was leaning under a bush nearby, digging a shallow hole with her hands. I watched nervously as she called for Tera and told him to hide under the bush, covering him with leaves. Then she moved on to another bush and called for Espoir. She was hiding us each under a separate bush.

I crawled toward Mama. "Let me hide with Tera! Or Espoir!" I begged.

Mama shook her head. "Together you'll make too much noise," she said.

"We won't make any noise!" I nearly shouted, and then I wished I hadn't spoken so loudly. I pictured Mama telling me to circle my tongue seven times.

Mama pointed under another bush. I dragged myself under the lonely branches, and Mama squatted next to me.

"Don't come out until you hear my voice again," she said firmly.

"Wait," I cried, and grabbed at her hand. Mama pulled back and pointed her chin toward the shrubs where Espoir and Tera were hidden.

"You're not alone," she said. "Your brothers are there."

I spun my head in a panic. From under the bush, I couldn't see Tera and Espoir. And anyway, I knew that they were too small to carry me. I wanted Mama. I wanted the smell of oil and soap on her skin. Only Mama could save me. And now she was leaving, going back down the hill.

I thought of the cries that we'd heard down the hill. The wooden spoon banging on a metal pot. "They're coming! They're coming," someone had warned. I didn't know who was coming, but now Mama was headed straight in that direction.

"You can't go down there," I begged.

Mama leaned close and pressed a finger to her lips. "Don't make any noise," she whispered. Then she was gone, and I was alone.

Chapter 13

I don't know how long we waited on top of Gapfura. I listened for the sound of Mama's feet, and her voice calling our names. But I couldn't hear anything—not even my brothers' breathing. All I could hear was the buzzing of insects. As time passed, I noticed baby birds chirping nearby. Their cries were small and feeble, and for the first time I didn't think about catching a bird and roasting the meat. I thought about those babies, waiting for their mother, like I was waiting for Mama.

I was overcome with horror. I'd never caught a bird myself. But Tera and my cousins had. "Bring me home a bird we can roast!" I'd often pleaded. I loved the taste of roasted bird. But now my stomach churned thinking of the birds we'd eaten. What if those birds were mothers? How long had their babies waited in their nest for a mother who would never return?

After a long time, I heard footsteps followed by a whisper. "Argentine. It's me," Mama was calling. I peered out from under the branches. Mama had returned! She was carrying a plastic bag with cooked beans. She whispered for my brothers to join us, and we gathered around the clump of beans.

I was so happy to see my mother that I couldn't stop asking questions. "Who did you see down there?" I chirped.

Mama said nothing.

"Did you see Aunt Kampire?" I asked again.

Mama shook her head.

"What about our cousins? Did you see Sifa?"

"No," Mama answered firmly.

"Well, who did you see?" I insisted. It seemed impossible that Mama had gone down the hill and seen no one. Where could everyone have gone?

"Eat quickly," Mama urged. As we were finishing the beans, a high-pitched cry rose from somewhere down the hill. "Yeeeeeeeeee! They're coming!"

Mama jumped to her feet. "Let's go," she said. I wondered how she knew who was shouting. What if it was a trick? What if we ran right into the arms of the attackers?

My brothers were already sliding down the hill on their backsides, hands and bare feet scraping the dirt. I slid behind them. Going downhill I was almost as fast as them. When we reached the bottom of the hill, we came to a dirt path. I was happy to see a place I recognized. This was the neighborhood where Aunt Kampire's brothers, Mpirikanye and Mavugo, lived.

But something was wrong. The familiar houses stood empty. There were no glowing fires—no smoke curling through the thatch roofs—no children playing outside. It was so quiet that not even a bird was singing. I glanced nervously from one empty house to the next, until I was afraid to look any further. *Where are all the people?* I wondered.

Mama pressed her finger to her lips. She yanked me onto her back again and grabbed Espoir and Tera, one on each hand. We sprinted across the empty footpath and into the banana plants below. Tera was in front, leading the way, but he didn't know where he was going. Soon he stopped and whipped his head frantically. "Mama, which way?" he cried. Mama shushed him and pointed further into the banana plants. Leaves brushed past my face.

The banana leaves reminded me of my father's side of the family. They lived in houses built onto the side of a hill, in a place where banana stalks grew thick in every direction. Usually, when we visited them, I stayed inside, unwilling to navigate the steep hills. But one year I had decided to follow my brothers into the banana stalks to see how banana beer was made. I crawled behind my brothers through a narrow path until we reached a clearing where the sweet scent of fermenting bananas and a warm hazy fire welcomed us. My parents, Aunt Kampire, and Uncle Manassé were gathered around a pile of yellow bananas, peeling and tossing them into a wooden trough where they'd be mashed into sweet juice. They were singing, telling stories, and roasting corn like a festival.

Now, as we swished through the banana stalks, it carried me back to that day. I could almost smell the smoky fire ahead and the sweet scent of fermenting bananas. But suddenly the rhythm of Mama's steps broke. We lurched forward, and I tumbled onto the cold, damp ground.

When I opened my eyes, Mama and I were lying in a shallow trench. One of our neighbors must have dug it on happier days, when they had been making banana beer. Now, the trench was empty, and we were sprawled on the ground.

Mama untied me from her back. I sat up, thankful to discover that I wasn't hurt. Then I looked at Mama. Her leg was twisted. My beautiful, strong mother couldn't stand up. My whole world disappeared in that moment. We'd never survive without Mama. She was our legs. She was our life. And now she couldn't stand.

"We'll stay here tonight." Mama winced, trying to make it sound as though we had a choice, but there was nothing else we could do. Espoir and Tera curled next to Mama, but I couldn't sleep. I needed my mother's legs more than I needed my own.

I stared at the leaves in front of me, hating myself. What kind of daughter was I? I was the oldest. I should have been carrying my brothers, but instead Mama had been carrying me. I was too heavy. I was nothing but a burden that Mama carried all her days.

I had to do something. I looked at the bushes and plants growing nearby. Leaves held cures. We all knew that. When my stomach felt sick, Mama made tea out of leaves. When I had a cold, she crushed eucalyptus leaves into our skin. Leaves were our medicine. If only I knew which plant could help Mama now. I started to pray as I crawled through the green leaves, touching one plant after another. I picked some leaves and crushed them between my fingers, then I returned to Mama and rubbed them onto her leg, praying fervently that my medicine would help her.

When morning came, Mama brushed the crushed leaves off her legs and gently pushed herself up. She gingerly hobbled forward. Her leg held. She was walking again. Joy rushed through my body. We were saved.

"Tugende. Let's go," Mama said as she reached for me. I leaned away, digging my fingernails into the soft soil beneath me.

"I'm too heavy," I said. "If you weren't carrying me, you wouldn't have fallen."

Mama stopped and shook her head. "My child, if you weren't praying for me, I wouldn't be standing."

Then she pulled me onto her back and led us further into the banana stalks.

Chapter 14

In the light of the morning, I realized that we weren't very far into the banana stalks. The previous night it had felt dark and closed in, but now I could see that the stalks were spaced far apart, and anyone could see us out here. We hiked further, until the banana stalks gave way to the pori—where bushes grew wild and tangled. I thought we were lost. Only now do I realize that these were the paths that Mama walked all the time, collecting firewood and hiking out to the fields. She must have known where we were, whose fields we were next to, and what other families might be seeking shelter nearby.

We reached a small clearing. "We'll sleep here," Mama declared and set me on the dark soil. The leaves were soft, half-rotting into the earth. We slept there that night, even though we had no fire and nothing to eat. In the darkness, I thought I could hear other children whimpering nearby.

The next day, it was clear that we were not going home. Mama squatted next to me. "I have to find food," she said quietly. This time I didn't cry out. I knew we needed the food.

When Mama returned, she brought sweet potatoes to roast. She sent my brothers to look for firewood nearby, but it was cold and moist in the pori. Espoir and Tera returned with sticks not yet dried out, branches that bent when you tried to break them. I hoped the sticks would light and the fire would catch before it was too late in the day. In the dark, I knew that we couldn't have a fire. A fire blazing at night would show everyone exactly where we were.

The next morning, Mama left again. This time she returned with a man walking beside her. At first, I thought it was our father. We hadn't seen him since we left our house. But instead, it was Mpirikanye, one of Aunt Kampire's brothers. Behind him, I could see his wife and three children, half-hidden by the trees. They must have been hiding somewhere nearby. It was as though the pori had become a village itself.

Mpirikanye was a tall, thin man with the softest voice I had ever heard. He said nothing about what had happened to his brother, but I remembered the way their houses had looked terribly empty when we'd crossed the path. Later I learned that his brother, Mavugo, had been beaten to death.

Mpirikayne said nothing about the things that had been done to his family. Instead, he built a small shelter out of branches for us, and another for his wife and children.

We stayed in those shelters for several nights. The adults would leave searching for food or checking to see if it was safe to return home. But one day Mama returned with a nervous look in her eyes. "It's not safe here," she said.

A knot formed in my stomach. I was comfortable where we were. The tangle of bushes had grown familiar. I was happy to have other children nearby. But Mama pointed to the leaves crushed on the ground. "Do you see our path?" she asked. "They'll see it too." And we ran again.

Chapter 15

We ran through banana stalks and fields planted with beans and cassava, until we reached a place called the kivumu. It was a dark forest of giant ficus trees, hidden deep in a valley. The trunks of the trees were so thick that no bullets could pass through.

When I saw those thick trees, I felt safe. But when Mama lowered me to the ground, it was cold and wet with dew that would never dry. Above us, there was no sky and no clouds, only heavy branches that creaked in the wind. The ground was covered with giant roots—sinewy and tangled, rising like vines. I pressed myself against the rough trunk of the tree. It buzzed with insects that I had never heard before.

We slept in the kivumu that night, and the next day my father arrived. He was carrying a large sack of beans across his shoulders. "So, this is where you are," he said to Mama.

I was surprised to see my father. To me, we were in a strange new place. But people run to the places they know, and my mother had run to the kivumu near our own fields. My father and Mpirikanye started bending sticks and building new shelters. When my father finished, he carefully stacked his sack of beans inside one of the shelters and turned to me. "You can stay here and guard the beans," he said. I shrank beside the heavy sack. It was twice as tall as me. How would I protect the beans? And who was going to protect me?

As soon as my father was gone, Mama scooped me up and carried me away from the shelter with the beans, until she found a hiding place for me under a thick, gnarly tree. "I'll come back soon," she said, looking at the branches as they scraped and creaked in the wind. I knew that Mama and Mpirikanye's wife, Bayavuge, were hiking to the fields to find something for us to eat.

When they returned a few hours later, I was confused. They were carrying ground sorghum to boil into a porridge. It didn't make sense. Where had they found ground sorghum? Another day they returned with cassava, already ground into flour. I began wondering where my mother was going.

Finally, Mama confessed. Bayavuge and Mama were creeping into empty villages, looking for a grinding rock or a mortar and pestle. I closed my eyes, and I pictured an empty village—doors broken open, houses ransacked, and two women grinding sorghum. What would happen if the attackers found them there?

When I was little, I often found my mother praying in our house. The rest of our family would be outside, and I would go back into our house looking for Mama. I'd crawl into a room and find my mother on her knees in a corner. *Look at those legs*, I would think. My mother was strong and beautiful, and I knew that if I had such good legs, I'd be running around. I'd never have the patience to stay in a corner and pray.

But now, in the kivumu, there was nothing left to do but pray. One morning, I was so desperate that I decided to fast and pray all day. Mama had hidden me under a giant tree and tucked an avocado next to me before she left for the day. I pushed the avocado away and started to pray. All morning, I fasted and prayed, but I was still a child and by the time the afternoon arrived, I had forgotten my own plans. My fingers stumbled on the avocado, and before I could even think about it, I was finishing the last bite and licking my fingers. Only then did I remember my plans to fast and pray.

Later that afternoon Mama returned to our hiding place with a neighbor from Shahalia. She must have met him along the way. The pori had morphed into a village again. Our neighbor stopped abruptly when he saw me tucked against the thick trunk of the tree.

"What have you done?" he gasped, looking at Mama. "Don't you know that these are the trees where the snakes live?"

I stared at the sinewy roots and thick vines. Only a little while earlier I had felt safe and hidden. Now my back prickled. Every part of the tree looked like a snake ready to wrap its long body around my neck.

It was all too much. How was I ever going to find a place to live in this world? I couldn't guard sacks of beans in the forest. And I couldn't sit under trees filled with snakes.

The next day I decided to fast and pray with new energy. I pushed away the roasted potato Mama had left for me and began to pray. This time, I didn't stop. I prayed, and I prayed until I was floating in a world of dreams. I dreamt that I was on a table, with people circling around me. They were looking at my legs. They wore white clothes, and I knew they were there to help me.

When Mama returned that afternoon, words spilled out of me. "Listen! Mama, I had a dream!" I cried. "I was lying on a table. There were people wearing white. They were touching my legs!"

Mama crouched next to me, listening carefully. We all knew that dreams held truth.

"Did you hear what the people were saying?" Mama asked slowly.

"No," I admitted. "But I heard a voice in my heart saying, humura—don't be afraid."

Days passed, or maybe it was weeks or months. We continued living in the kivumu, but my mind stayed in that dream. I couldn't stop thinking of those people in white. In the kivumu, there was nothing white. We couldn't even see the white of the clouds. Everything was green and brown. I started thinking of Pastor Amani, how he had visited us in Shahalia, in the days before we started running. I thought of the place he told us about—the Centre Pour Handicapés—the place with girls like me.

Suddenly, I understood. I had dreamt about the Centre Pour Handicapés in Goma. I knew there would be doctors there, and I knew they would be wearing white.

"We have to go to Goma!" I insisted. "I saw it in my dream!"

Chapter 16

As I was sitting in the kivumu talking about my dream, I didn't know that Mama had already taken me to the Centre Pour Handicapés in Goma when I was only two years old. As we sat in the kivumu, Mama must have been circling her tongue in her mouth, unwilling to dismiss my dream and cut the only hope I had found.

There were so many things Mama didn't say at that time, so many doors she had knocked on without finding an answer. "God saved us in Mweso," was the only thing I had ever heard her say about the town where I was born. Only later would she tell me more of the story.

I was born in Mweso—a town much bigger than the village of Shahalia. In Mweso, there was a market, and a hospital, and a road full of holes. I was my parents' first child—a baby like any other baby. At one year old, I had a head full of hair and was starting to walk. Then I got sick. Mama carried me to the hospital, then carried me back home. For weeks my illness continued. Until one night, my skin burned so hot that Mama could barely touch me. It was dark in Mweso. There was no electricity or phone—only Mama's prayers. She prayed through the night, and when morning came, I was still alive. My skin had cooled, and I was smiling.

Mama thanked God. Then she tried to stand me up, and my legs collapsed like water beneath me.

Mama carried me back to the doctors in Mweso. "It's polio—she'll never walk—you're lucky she is alive," they said.

But Mama wasn't satisfied with that answer. "How will a child like this survive in the world?" she asked. When the doctors offered no answer, Mama started to reason with God. "If only my child could walk, or even just crawl, at least she could pull herself out of the rain."

Every day, Mama fasted and prayed and pleaded with God, until one day she grew so weak that her knees began to wobble. "A little water will help," she said to herself. Then she laid me on a mat in the house and walked to the river nearby.

The rivers in Mweso are strong and dirty, picking up everything along the way. Mama stood in that river, and the current pulled her legs. Suddenly, she fell, and water rushed toward her. She almost went under until she remembered me, lying on a thatch mat in the house. A house that often flooded. A child who couldn't pull herself out of the rain.

"God, if I die what will happen to my child?" Mama cried. Then, like a miracle, she was out of the water, walking back up the hill, believing she had seen death and survived. Mama carried me to the church that day and testified that God had saved both our lives.

Soon after that, my brother Tera was born.

"Focus on the new baby," my father said.

But by this time, I was two years old, and Mama had heard about the Centre Pour Handicapés in Goma. It was one hundred kilometers away over a dangerous road. Mama was a young wife with two small children and no money at all. But soon she found a friend going to Goma. Together, the two women traveled with me and Tera on the back of a truck.

When we arrived at the Centre Pour Handicapés, the doctors looked skeptically at me. "She's too young. Come back in a few years. Come back with money next time," they said.

And Mama returned to my father, with nothing to show for her journey.

Soon after that, Espoir was born. By the time I was five, my parents had three children, and fighting had started in Mweso. People were saying one to another, "We'll kill them all and throw them into the river."

That's when we left Mweso, the town where I was born—with the hospital, and river and road full of holes.

It must have been hard for my parents, carrying a girl who couldn't walk, and two small boys into the hills, to a village so small that we'd never see a doctor, or even a motorcycle. But that is what my parents wanted—a place where we could disappear—where the war might never find us.

But now, five years later, we were sitting in the kivumu with sacks of beans. There was no road back to the town of Mweso, or to the Centre Pour Handicapés in the city of Goma. We were stuck in the kivumu with only my dream.

"Mama, I had a dream! Let's go to Goma!" I chirped, as we sat under those trees filled with snakes.

And Mama must have circled her tongue seven times.

Chapter 17

Eventually we left the kivumu, but we didn't go to Goma, despite my dream. Instead, we returned to our house in Shahalia where we continued to live in wasiwasi, the place of worries.

My third brother, Ushindi, was born after we returned to our house. His name means victory, as though my father was hoping for an end to the war, victory for someone. But there was no end to the fighting that had seized our hills, even I could see that.

My fear of war was matched only by my fear of losing my mother. On the day Ushindi was born, my mother closed the door to her room and sent me outside, where I circled our house, praying. When I crawled back inside, my eye caught on a bloody kitenge, and my heart left my stomach. Cold flooded my body. But when I saw Ushindi's small face, all my fears fell away.

I washed my hands carefully, scrubbing away every crumble of dirt. Then, when my hands were clean, I took the baby into my arms. Tera and Espoir called for our neighbors and paraded from house to house singing cherere and collecting eggplant and sweet potatoes in a basin. That is what the children in our village did every time a new baby was born. It was a way of gathering gifts for the family. Everyone in the village gave something. We might have been a village lost in a war, but we were still a village, and we needed our neighbors more than ever.

Around this time, I noticed that something else had changed in Shahalia. There were children I'd never seen before. They passed from house to house asking for food or clothes. I felt sorry for those children. They had thin faces and skin that needed oil rubbed on it. I knew our family didn't have much, but I could tell that we had more than these children. Whenever I saw them, I'd whisper, "Come to our house. My mother will give you bananas and avocados."

Sometimes those children arrived at our door, and we had nothing to share. But even then, Mama would tell them to return with their mothers, and together Mama and the women would hike cautiously out to our fields to find something to harvest.

"Who are they?" I asked Mama when we were alone.

"They came from Rwanda," she answered, her voice still.

"But what is Rwanda?"

"It is a country nearby," Mama answered.

"But why? Why are they here? Why did they leave their country?" I asked, desperate to understand their uprooted lives in ways that I couldn't understand my own.

Mama raised her eyebrows, and I thought she was going to tell me to circle my tongue, but instead, she answered with a question of her own. "When you look at their faces, what do you see?"

I closed my eyes and tried to imagine the women, but all I could see was their neatly cropped hair and their long flowing skirts that reached to their ankles.

"Think again," Mama prompted. "Can't you see? Their faces are still shiny. Where they came from, they had something. Now they have nothing."

I was still a child. I didn't know anything about the war or the ways it was shifting. What I understood were the children, with their dry faces and their unfocused eyes. We were all living in wasiwasi now.

Chapter 18

In the night, I heard bullets crying. I hated the sound of those bullets. It made me feel sick. "Are there places where bullets don't cry?" I would ask Mama.

"Yes, there are countries where people have peace," Mama would answer.

"But why not our country?" I'd ask.

I never got an answer to that.

Sometimes, Mama cooked early in the afternoon. "Hurry, eat quickly," she said, as her eyes traveled over the hills. When evening came, we slid into the banana stalks to hide until morning. On other nights, we stayed in our house and slept in our prayers. We slept in layers of clothing, ready to run with as much as we could.

But sometimes there was no chance to run. The attackers came in the pounding rain, so that we couldn't hear the warning cries of our neighbors. They switched off their flashlights and came during mbala mwezi, the light of the moon guiding their way.

One night, we were lying on our mats, when our wooden door thudded open. Bright light burned my eyes.

At first, I couldn't see anything.

Then I saw my father—trapped under the table—a gun pointed at his head.

A knife pressed to Ushindi's small stomach.

"Give us your money, or we'll kill him," a voice threatened. I squeezed my eyes shut. I was afraid even to cough.

On that night, my father gave the men money, and they let us live. But they came back again and again. Or maybe it was different men who came. But they all said the same thing. "You better have more money next time."

They took our pots and our food. They took the used clothes my father sold at the market. They took my special blanket.

Until one morning, I looked around our empty house and realized there was nothing more these men could steal. There was nothing left for them to take but our lives.

Chapter 19

In between those attacks, life continued. The following year, Mama gave birth to another baby, my brother Soleil. His name means sun. But he was born sick, and Mama spent the months that followed his birth hiking from one healer to another, looking for someone to cure him.

I was the oldest child and the only girl, and I desperately wanted to do something to help Mama.

On market day, I'd sit outside our house, watching the footpath fill with people and wishing I could be one of those people on the way to the market. There were men pushing chukudus piled high with heavy sacks of potatoes and onions. There were girls balancing bundles of casava leaves. Everyone would be carrying something. I was fascinated by those sweating bodies—the narrow shoulders that carried so much weight.

If I sat outside of our house all day, those same people would return in the afternoon. On the way home from the market, people looked different. They smiled and greeted each other. They carried small bags of oil and salt. Children ran toward their parents, asking if they'd brought any candy. With all my heart, I wished I could be one of those people, returning from the market, with something to offer my family. If only I could be the one to bring home the salt and the oil. But the market in Kachenje was far away, and I knew it was a place I'd never visit.

Mama must have seen my frustration, because she suggested that I start selling mutobe—mashed banana juice—from our house. I didn't think anyone would buy mutobe from me. Ever since I was little, I had been aware of my hands that wouldn't stay clean. At my aunt's house, I had overheard one of my cousins talking about my hands. "I don't want to share food with Argentine. Her hands are always dirty," my cousin had complained, and my aunt had silenced him sharply. But those words still hung in my head. Would a stranger really buy mutobe from me? There were adults in Shahalia who wouldn't even shake my hand.

Mama bought glass bottles and filled each one with fresh banana juice. "Self-serve mutobe," she said. I hung a green banana leaf by the side of the path, like a sign.

"Hodi," my first customer called.

"Karibu," I answered from where I was sitting on my mat, my legs bent to one side.

"Ehh...you? Are you the one selling mutobe?" the man asked, as he blinked in the dim light and caught sight of me on the floor.

I drew in a breath. "Yes, it's me," I answered, hiding my hands. I nodded toward the table. "Don't worry, you can serve yourself," I explained.

The man squinted at me in confusion. But it was hot outside, and he must have been thirsty. After a breath, he shrugged, wiped his hands on his pants, and reached for a bottle. He drank the juice then paid me. I had sold my first bottle of sweet, fresh mutobe, and I was proud to be helping Mama.

Chapter 20

One evening, we were gathered around the cooking fire inside our house. Bottles of mutobe were stacked in the corner, ready for the next day. My father wasn't home yet, and Mama hadn't even blocked our door shut.

Suddenly we heard shouting.

"Run! They're coming!" a neighbor yelled.

We weren't ready to run. A look of panic flashed across Mama's face. Then she remembered to smooth her expression.

Mama stood up. She grabbed Soleil and tied him onto her back. Then she turned toward the rest of us. She reached for Ushindi with one hand and Espoir with another.

That left me and Tera—the two oldest children.

Mama did the only thing that she could. She turned to Tera. "Stay with your sister," she said as she ran out of the house with Soleil, Ushindi, and Espoir.

Tera and I didn't move. *Maybe we should follow Mama,* I thought. But, before I could do anything, a man appeared in the doorway. He had a long green coat and big black boots, and he carried a gun. It was too late to follow Mama now.

I backed away from the fire, hoping the man wouldn't see me. I was small, and I was used to people looking right past me. But this man took out a flashlight and spiraled the beam through our house until it landed on me. Bright light burned my eyes.

"There you are!" the large man exclaimed, pointing the beam directly into my eyes. "Where is your mother?" he asked.

Mama. I thought, then I pinched my lips shut. I spun my tongue in circles. *Before you take a word out of your mouth, circle your tongue seven times*, I told myself, just like Mama always told me.

She couldn't have gone very far. She was probably hiding in the banana stalks by the side of our house. She'd be pressing Soleil to her chest trying to shush him.

"Where is your mother?" the man repeated.

"I don't know," I whispered tentatively.

The man looked at me, then he shrugged and turned toward the door. When I looked in that direction, my heart left my stomach. Hovering in the doorway were more men with trench coats and tall, black boots. They stomped into our house and took off their backpacks. Their guns clanked against their supplies.

The large man with the flashlight turned back to me. "Look at you," he breathed slowly. "You are a good girl, aren't you?" His lips curled into a smile. The light from his flashlight slid down my body and jerked to a stop. "What's wrong with your legs?" he demanded.

"I am disabled," I answered.

There was a pause, and the man pointed his flashlight back at my face. "Never mind about that. Come here by the fire," he said, patting the dirt floor beneath him.

I crawled out of the dark corner as slowly as I could. Tera moved with me.

"Don't be afraid. We won't kill you," the man said, glancing briefly at Tera, then returning his gaze to me.

As I crawled forward, the man leaned into the fire so that his face glowed in the light. I squeezed my eyes shut. "Look at me," he demanded. "Do you recognize me?"

I didn't want to look at this man. I didn't want to know who he was. All my life, Mama had told me to hide. "You have to be ready to throw yourself down the hill and into the bushes," she'd say. Now here I was, caught out in the open.

"I don't know who you are," I mumbled without looking up. I tried to arrange my voice the way Mama arranged her face—calm and blank like a rock.

"Are you sure you don't know me?" the man asked again. When I shook my head, he continued. "You must hear what they say in the village. Tell me—who do they say that we are?"

Interahamwe. I thought. But I couldn't say that.

The man leaned closer. "What do they say that we do?"

I knew I had to say something. I opened my mouth. "Some say that you kill people," I started, then choked on my words. "But I don't know—I've never seen that."

The man stared at me. His face was very still. I looked away. In the corner of the room, I saw stalks of cooking bananas that the other men had dragged into our house.

"Maybe you bring bananas for people to eat," I offered.

The man's face cracked into a smile. He laughed and handed me a stalk of bananas. "Help me peel these."

I took the bananas he offered me and picked up a small knife that was resting by the fire. I started to peel the green bananas, as I stole a glance at the door. It was open again, and there were even more men outside. I thought about Mama, Soleil, Ushindi and Espoir, shaking under the banana leaves. What would the men do if they found my mother hidden there?

Inside, the men were shuffling through our pots and dishes, taking whatever they wanted. They found my bottles of mutobe and started to drink. The large man reached inside his backpack and brought out tins of tomato paste and a bag of peanut flour. Then he took out a thick, black book. He turned back to me and started asking his questions again.

"Tell me, am I a good person or a bad person?"

I didn't stop to think about my answer this time. "You are a good person," I said, looking nervously at the black book in his hand. It looked like a Bible.

"Ahhh...Yes! Maybe I am a good person." The man laughed, his teeth flashing under his smile. He held the black book to the light. "Maybe I am a pastor. Come here, let me teach you about God." He smiled and patted the floor again.

I pretended to move closer, and the man opened the Bible and started to talk. In the shadows, the other men were eating and lying on the floor. But this man kept talking—the Bible clutched in his hands.

When the fire grew low, the man declared that it was time to sleep for the night. "Take your brother and sleep in the other room. In the morning, we will be gone," he instructed. I started to crawl out of the room. The knot in my stomach loosened. Maybe the man wouldn't hurt us. Maybe he *was* a good man.

Suddenly the man hissed. "Wait. Come back. You must do one thing for me."

I stopped. Dread rose in my throat. Tera had already vanished into the other room. It was just me with this man. I turned slowly around and crawled back toward the fire.

The room was quiet, except for the heavy breathing of the other men as they slept. When I reached the fire again, the large man studied me. My skin rippled cold. He nodded his chin toward my legs. "We didn't hurt you today." He coughed, cleared his throat, and stared back at my face. "But not every man will be good like us."

I didn't say anything.

He continued. "You have to do something for me." I lowered my eyes wishing I could crumble myself into pieces on the floor. I felt like a child, hiding in the bushes and listening to the cows chomping nearby. I was sure to be crushed.

The man dropped his voice to a whisper. "When your mother returns, tell her to never leave you alone again."

That was all he said. I nodded, and he waved me away.

When I reached the bedroom, I huddled next to Tera. My body was shaking. I still didn't know what this man wanted, and I didn't dare close my eyes. I lay there, staring into the darkness, my body tense and ready to leap. After a long time, I heard the clicking of metal and the heavy thud of boots as the men left our house.

Still, I tried not to move. "Don't come out until you hear my voice calling your name," Mama always said. I thought of the story that she used to tell us, about the mother bird who leaves her babies in a nest. All the other animals come and try to mimic the song of that mother bird. The frog. The snake. The hawk. "I'm your mother. I'm here," they sing. But those baby birds aren't fooled. They know the sound of their mother's voice.

Finally, Mama arrived. She tiptoed into the house and fell to her knees when she saw us. "God be praised! You are alive!" was all that she said.

Chapter 21

After that night, Mama became even more worried. It was like a test she couldn't pass correctly. There was no way she could protect us all, and now she was pregnant again.

In desperation, my parents abandoned our house and took us to live with my father's parents in a cluster of huts built on the side of a hill, where the air was drenched with the scent of crushed, rotting bananas. I couldn't sell mutobe in those huts. No one walked by. There was not a single neighbor close enough for me to visit. It was a world so steep that I couldn't even crawl out the door. I sat in a dark corner of one of those huts, watching my grandfather and his wives suck banana beer out of a gourd, their voices escalating until they erupted angrily at each other.

My fifth brother, Bonheur, was born in those huts on the hill. He died only a few months after he was born. Soleil was still sick and, after Bonheur died, Mama returned Soleil to her back like a baby. She must have felt like she was losing everything.

I couldn't stop thinking about the way my body was changing. I was eleven, and I was starting to grow breasts like a woman. But the rest of my body was going in the other direction. My legs had curled up, the muscles atrophied. My back curved more every day. Maybe if I hadn't leaned so much, I could have stayed straight. Now, it was too late. In those huts on the hill, I felt like I might vanish into the earth.

Eventually, we returned to our house on the footpath in Shahalia, where I was able to sit outside again. But now, I felt strangely exposed. One day, I was sitting by our house, watching people walk by, when a skinny boy appeared before me. He wasn't from Shahalia, but I had seen him playing with some of our neighbors. The boy stared at me. Then, without saying anything, he reached low and touched my chest, then jumped up and ran away, a sly smile on his face.

My heart raced. *Why did he do that? What does he want from me?*

That night, I considered what I should do. I didn't want to tell Mama. Soleil was still sick, and I didn't want to add to her worries. I could have told Tera and Espoir. But they were younger than me. Tera was slow with his words. Espoir was fast, but he was still young. I was growing older. For Mama's sake, I wanted to handle the situation myself.

The next time I saw that skinny boy, he was walking down the dirt path with his friends. I crawled toward Aunt Kampire's house. The boy pretended not to see me. He stopped to kick a ball made from banana leaves. He smirked at me, then feigned innocence. All the while, he was coming closer and closer.

Suddenly he was in front of me, arms dangling down to touch me again. I lunged at his legs, like I used to tackle my brothers when we were younger. Pah. The skinny boy fell to the ground. His friends shouted in surprise. I grabbed onto the boy and refused to let go.

Aunt Kampire heard the shouting and rushed over. "What is this?" she cried, trying to pull us apart. But I wouldn't let go.

"Why did you touch me?" I spat the words out. "Say it! What do you want from me?"

The boy refused to say anything, and I kept clinging to him. More women came. Someone pulled the boy away and brought him back to his parents. I heard he was beaten by his father that night.

I saw that boy a few times after that, and he never bothered me again. When he saw me, he lowered his head and walked in a different direction. But I couldn't help wondering what would have happened if that boy had been bigger. I thought of my father telling me to guard that sack of beans in the ki-vumu. I wanted to cross my arms over my chest and ask, *who will guard me?*

At night, I heard Mama speaking softly to my father. "We have to go now. If we wait any longer, it will be too late." Mama wanted to take me to the Centre Pour Handicapés in Goma. She'd never forgotten my dream.

But every time my mother brought up the subject, my father dismissed her.

"I must try. I must do something," Mama would say.

"Goma's far away," my father would answer. "It's a big city. You'll get lost. You have no money. Even if you make it to the Centre, those doctors will send you back home again."

My father would list one obstacle after another. But no matter how many times he tried to carry my mother off to the left or off to the right, my mother kept standing there—determined to march straight ahead—all the way to the city of Goma. Finally, my father relented.

"Go if you want," he shrugged, "but you might as well be hanging yourself."

My mother didn't wait for my father to say anything else. She started preparing for our journey. First, Mama brought four-year-old Ushindi to stay with her mother in Nyanzale. Then she brought Espoir to stay with my grandfather, the pastor, on his farm where the tea was milky and sweet. Tera would stay in Shahalia with my father. Only Soleil would go with us. He was too young and too sick to leave behind.

Underneath her calm face, my mother must have been closing her heart, tying it shut again, so none of her fears could fall out. "I'll come back soon," she must have told my brothers, just like she'd always told all of us.

I packed a few clothes, oil for my skin, and soap. I was ready to go. This was the opportunity I had been waiting for all my life. There was only one thing that bothered me. "What gift can I bring for those who will receive us?" I asked Mama.

"Bring the mats that you weave," she answered.

In our village, to give someone a thatch mat was to give them something of value. We used mats to sleep on at night, to sit on outside, and to kneel on in prayer. I rolled up two mats that I had woven. One was for Ma Mukubwa, my mother's older sister who lived in Goma, and another was for Pastor Amani's wife. I was sure that one day we'd see Pastor Amani again. We were headed toward my dream, and I knew God would carry us there.

Part II

Hope

Chapter 22

The journey to Goma would be long, Mama told me. We would hike through the banana stalks and swamp, and over the hills until we reached Mweso—the town where I was born. Then we had to find a way from Mweso to Goma, a hundred kilometers over a dangerous road. "We might not make it. We might have to return home," Mama warned. I nodded thoughtfully, but in my heart, I knew I'd never return to Shahalia.

In preparation for our departure, Mama went to our church to talk to the pastor. He and his wife had always been kind to us. Their quiet daughter, Magambo, had helped carry me on those choir trips. They also had two boys only a little older than me, Ruberiti and Rupyisi. When Mama explained her plans, the pastor's wife offered to send her sons to walk with us on the first day of the journey.

Mama thanked the family for their kindness and looked at the boys. She must have been trying to imagine how far they could carry us. Ruberiti and Rupyisi were thin with narrow shoulders, and Mweso was a full day's walk from Shahalia, even for strong men like my father. If Ruberiti and Rupyisi grew tired and turned back too soon, Mama would be left in the pori with me and Soleil, two children who couldn't walk.

Ruberiti and Rupyisi arrived at our house the next morning. They brought a chukudu. Ndahimana, an older boy from my father's side of the family, also arrived, and he looked strong.

I climbed on the chukudu, and the boys tied my mats onto the side of the wooden scooter. Mama carried a bundle of clothes and food on her head. On her back, she tied Soleil.

"Argentine, the journey is long, and there are many dangers," Mama warned again.

"Yes, Mama," I answered, bowing my head. I was already sitting on the chukudu, facing forward, with my legs wrapped around the steering pole.

The boys began to push, and I held onto the chukudu as it rolled forward in the dirt. The path was bumpy, and my legs kept slipping off. I used one hand to hold my legs in place as I had on those trips home from school. But I was older now, and my back had grown weaker, not stronger. As we moved downhill, the chukudu started rolling faster. I spun my head, trying to keep sight of Mama. The thought of losing her terrified me.

"Let's wait for Mama," I begged the boys, and they pulled the chukudu back and waited patiently. When Mama arrived, they began pushing forward again.

On the path, there were many people. Some of them greeted us pleasantly, but others stood by the side of the road, staring at me. "Uriya baramujyanyehe koko?" they muttered. "Honestly, where can you be taking that girl?" they asked, as though I was too small and too sick to merit carrying anywhere. I closed my heart and continued looking forward.

My eyes fell on Ruberiti, Rupyisi, and Ndahimana. Who were these boys? They were the opposite of the people muttering by the side of the road. They were offering me a kindness that I could never repay. Every time I begged them to go slower, they pulled themselves back and waited patiently for Mama to reach us.

In front of us, I saw beautiful, bright green plants, growing out of black mud. "Is this the mukangu?" I asked. Mama had told me about the place of the swamp—where men's legs sank in the mud. Now Ndahimana's legs were covered in dark mud. There was no way he could push me on the chukudu any further.

Ndahimana asked if he could carry me. Then he lifted me off the chukudu and pulled me onto his back. He took a step. First his feet disappeared, and then his ankles, then part of his legs. As he continued forward, I felt us sinking into the softness, but the mud didn't touch me. We reached dry earth again. Ndahimana set me on the ground and waded back to the other side, where Ruberiti and Rupyisi stood with the chukudu. Ndahimana lifted the chukudu above his head. Ruberiti and Rupyisi followed along with Mama who was still balancing the bundle on her head and Soleil on her back.

When everyone was on dry earth, I sat on the chukudu, and we continued forward. We were surrounded by banana plants on both sides of the path. The plants were pressed together, thick and dark. Suddenly we rolled around a curve and a steep hill appeared before us. There were dirt steps cut into the cliff. I had never seen a hill so steep and so high before. The dew from the surrounding banana plants had formed streams of water that slid down the slippery steps.

"Argentine, can you climb this cliff?" Ndahimana asked.

My heart jumped into my throat. We'd never make it. We'd already failed. There was no way I could climb this steep hill.

Ndahimana broke into a grin and a soft chuckle. "Don't worry. We'll go around," he said, pointing into the banana plants. Between the green leaves, I could see a narrow path. Relief flooded over me.

The path through the banana stalks was not as steep as the stairs, but it was narrow, as though not many people passed through there. The leaves were wet with dew, and soon I was shaking with cold. We didn't see any other people walking on the path.

I prayed that Ruberiti, Rupyisi, and Ndahimana would keep pushing, even though I knew they were tired. They could have left us. They could have looked around at the growing darkness and said, "We must go home now. Our mother is expecting us." But they kept going, and finally we came out of the banana stalks and onto a road. In the distance, I could see a stretch of land, caught between hills.

"That's Mweso," Mama said. As we approached, I saw a river ahead. This was the town where I was born. But we had left when I was five, and I didn't remember ever living here. Mama twisted her neck, searching for something. She pointed at a row of mud houses. "That's Majinaa's house," she said.

Mama had told me about Majinaa, our neighbor in Mweso. "Majinaa held Tera's hands and taught him to walk," she'd explained. I couldn't remember Tera ever being that small. In my mind, he'd always been able to walk.

We stopped in front of a mud house. The woman sitting outside leapt to her feet.

"Mama Argentine? Is that you? Are we meeting again?" she asked my mother, and they embraced. I had climbed off the chukudu and was sitting on the ground, trying to wipe the dirt from my hands.

Children were starting to form a circle around me. "Look at that crippled girl," one of them said. "Look at the way she walks on her hands!" In that moment I wanted to go back to Shahalia, where everyone already knew me.

Majinaa welcomed us into her house. Ndahimana, Ruberiti, and Rupyisi followed us inside. It was late in the day—long past the time the boys should have returned home.

Mama opened her bundle tied with a kitenge and took out roasted taro root, avocados, and cooked beans. "You must eat before you return," she said to the boys. They ate quickly and stood to leave.

"God bless you! We'll see you again!" they said to me, and they were off, pushing the chukudu over the muddy road full of holes.

"Mama, how will we know if they arrive safely?" I asked, looking at the fading light and thinking of the bullets that cried in the night. I remembered the stories of boys who were caught pushing chukudus too far from home. No one ever knew if they'd been killed or carried into the pori to fight.

"We'll pray for them," Mama said, as their shapes vanished into the hills.

Chapter 23

We slept at Majinaa's house that night. The air was cold and wet, and morning came heavy with mist.

"Is it always like this in Mweso?" I asked my mother.

"Ehh! Don't you remember?" Mama chuckled. "Now they have trenches, but when we lived in Mweso, the river was always so full that it would vomit water into the streets. I scooped water out of our house with a dish."

"Is that why we left?" I asked.

Mama said nothing.

Outside I heard the laughter of children. I crawled to the doorway and saw the soft shapes of children playing in the mist. They stopped and stared at me, open-mouthed.

"There she is," a girl whispered, pointing at me.

"Look at her legs," another said.

I tucked my legs underneath me, wishing I could sink into the ground, the way Ndahimana's boots had sunk into the mud. More children pressed toward me. Their faces cut through the heavy air and materialized before me suddenly sharp. I scrambled into the house and pulled the door shut behind me. On the other side of the dim room, my mother was talking to Majinaa.

"I'm going to take Argentine back to Goma," my mother explained as she lifted one of my woven mats and showed it to Majinaa.

"Argentine, did you weave this yourself? Congratulations! You're really growing up," Majinaa said. But I wasn't feeling grown up. I was trying to remember myself as a young child—trying to carry myself back to the baby I must have been, here in Mweso, where the houses were always flooding, and the river carried away everything we had.

Mama stood and started toward the door. "I must go. Be ready in case I return soon," she said to me.

My mother had no money, but she had a plan. Goma was one hundred kilometers away, and we could not pay for a bus ticket. We couldn't even pay for a ride on a Fuso—the heavy trucks that traveled between Mweso and Goma. But one of my mother's sisters, Ma Mukubwa, lived in Goma. Her husband worked on a Fuso that traveled from Goma through Mweso to a village called Kashuga. That Fuso was our only chance.

Mama had told me about this back in Shahalia as she watched the sorghum grow—green stalks changing to red flowery heads. In harvest season Fuso trucks traveled from Goma to Masisi to load up on sorghum, corn, and sweet potatoes to bring back to the city. We wanted to be part of that harvest. "If we go now, your uncle's truck will pass by," Mama had said. "Maybe he'll give us a ride to Goma."

The plan was for my mother to stand by the side of the road. She'd stand there every day searching for my uncle's Fuso, hoping one day it would pass. If the truck arrived, we would have no time to prepare. We had to be ready to go.

Mama walked out the door and into the mist. "Be patient. It could take weeks," she said to me. Only a little while later, she came running back into the house, with Soleil bumping up and down on her back.

"I found Beauf (beau-frère)!" Mama exclaimed. "Let's go fast!"

"But did you tell him about me?" I asked, dropping my head, suddenly nervous. I remembered the way those children had stared at me, and I wasn't sure if my uncle knew anything about me.

Mama was grabbing our clothes and stuffing them into a bundle as she moved toward the door. "Beauf is loading the truck at the depot. He'll be back soon," she said, without answering my question.

I scrambled to follow my mother. Outside, the mist had burned away, and I could see that the road was filled with holes and rocks. "We have to go there," Mama said, nodding down the road. "Can you carry yourself?"

I was already tying fabric onto my hands and my knees, wrapping the cloth in swirls like snakes. I was going to crawl down the road as fast as I could, even if everyone stared at me. If we missed my uncle, it would be a long time before he returned, and I did not want to stay in Mweso any longer.

I said a quick goodbye to Majinaa and crawled down the road, one arm after another, my head thrusting forward from the effort. The sun was hot now. I was so close to the ground that I could feel the heat radiating off the broken pavement. I crawled, and I crawled, until we stopped on the side of the road.

"Your uncle said to wait here," Mama informed me. I looked around and saw other people standing nearby with bundles balanced on their hands or resting at their feet. Everyone was speaking Swahili, loud and fast, and I couldn't remember the words anymore, but I was happy. We'd be leaving soon.

As I sat by the edge of the road, I heard a roar so deep it shook the ground. It was a Fuso—a truck—thundering toward us. The tires were giant, twice as tall as me. As the truck rolled by, I became a little girl again, pinching my eyes shut, trying not to see the danger. I scrambled back, away from the edge of the road. That tire would crush me—grind me into a powder.

After the Fuso faded into the distance, I peered up at Mama. "Will our Fuso be big like that?"

"Ours will be bigger," Mama answered gently.

"But...aren't there any small Fusos?" I begged.

"Not for us," Mama answered. Soleil was starting to squirm on her back, and she slid him to her chest.

Another Fuso roared by. This one was even bigger. The back of the Fuso was piled with giant sacks, one on top of another. All those days in Shahalia, when I had watched our dirt path fill with people carrying goods to the market, I had seen only people on foot and men pushing chukudus. Sometimes, I saw a bicycle. I had never imagined these trucks. They were so tall and so loud. They were monstrous. I'd never survive.

I wanted to go home—back to Shahalia, back through the swamp and the banana stalks, back to a world where I could travel by chukudu. If I fell off a chukudu, there was a chance I'd survive. But if I fell from one of these terrible trucks, I knew I'd be crushed.

I gulped in the air and almost choked. It was bitter, filled with fumes. Another Fuso rumbled past and heaved to a stop. "This is it," Mama said. I looked at the truck groaning nearby. It was packed high with a tower of sacks and covered with tarps and ropes.

Strong men jumped off the Fuso. I watched as they tied things to the side. Rolled-up foam mattresses, water jugs, and charcoal grills dangled in all directions.

Someone brought a ladder made from branches and leaned it onto the back of the truck, and I watched in horror as the people nearby started clambering up the thin, wobbly ladder to the top of the truck. They were sitting on top of the sacks, ready to fall off at any moment. *I can't go up there*, I thought. *My God. How will I ever survive?*

My eyes scrambled to the front of the Fuso. There was a cabin for the truck driver. It was lower to the ground. It looked safe and solid. Maybe they'd make room for me in there. I could sit next to the driver. I was small. I'd hardly take any space.

My uncle turned and looked at Mama. "Where is that girl of yours?" he asked.

"She's over there," Mama answered.

My uncle called for one of the strong men to pick me up, and we moved toward the front of the truck. I was sure he was carrying me to the cabin, where I could sit next to the driver, but instead, the man stopped short. Behind the cabin was a place where men were standing on top of the truck with their arms hanging down. "Raise her up," someone called.

My heart stopped. Cold flooded my body. They were going to lift me to the top of the truck, where I was sure to fall off. I'd be blown away in the wind. I took a breath and tried to calm my face. If my uncle saw my fear, he might leave me behind. And I had no other options. This was the only way forward, even if it was on the top of a Fuso.

The man hoisted me above his head, like a sack of potatoes or a rolled-up mattress. The world spun. Hands reached down. Someone grabbed hold of me. I was passed from one set of hands to another. Finally, I reached the top of the truck, where passengers were sitting.

"That one! She'll never be able to hold on," a woman dismissed. I thought of myself on the chukudu in Shahalia. The path had been so bumpy that I couldn't hold on. How would I ever hold on now?

"Pass her over here," another passenger offered.

There were more hands, and I found myself settled between people whose faces I could not recognize. I was high on top of the truck, and there was nothing to hold onto and nowhere to rest my sore back. I tried to sink between shoulders. Mama climbed next to me. She had Soleil in her arms.

When the truck started to move, I turned to Mama, "How long will we ride on this Fuso?"

"Not long. Maybe a few days," Mama shrugged.

The blood in my body ran cold again. "You mean all night? We'll sit on this truck all night?"

I knew it was dangerous. I was thinking of Shahalia, the way parents called their children inside before dark. *"Mwenye haana kwabo, alale mu muti,"* they sang. *"He who has no home, sleep in a tree."* Now we would be the ones with no home, sleeping in a tree.

"Pray for us, Argentine," Mama said softly. "God will protect us."

The engine of the truck rumbled, and we jerked forward. *Dear God, may I never return this way again,* I prayed. I felt dizzy watching the sky move above us. When the truck slowed, I started to calm. But then the truck leaned hard to one side as it lumbered into a ditch. I felt my body sway and grabbed onto the clothes of the stranger sitting next to me.

Below, I could hear women shouting from the side of the road, "You're going to get stuck there!" they warned our driver.

"We're lucky it's not rainy season," Mama murmured as we traveled on. The truck was vibrating so deeply that I felt it in my stomach.

Suddenly, we thudded to a stop. Something was wrong with our Fuso. I could hear the strong men leaping down and climbing under our vehicle. I had hated this towering truck, but now I clung to it desperately. I realized that I had nowhere else to go. If the strong men couldn't fix our truck, the other passengers could hike back to the villages we'd passed along the way. But my fate was stuck on this machine, and it was growing dark and cold.

After a long time, we started rolling forward again. I was relieved to be moving, except that now we were pitching forward into pure darkness. Only the light from our headlights filled the ditches ahead. It felt like we were rolling toward the end of the world.

Just as I was closing my heart, the other passengers began to sing. Slowly their voices rose, covering the terrible rumble of the engine. Their song lit the darkness. It soldered the pieces of my heart back together. And there, in that moment, I began to hope. Maybe we were going to live. Maybe we'd make it to Goma. Maybe I'd never have to travel this road again.

Soon we reached an area where there were no trees. The land was dark and wide open, and the wind whipped across the top of the truck and through our clothes. "This is Kilo-lirwe," Mama said. She told me how we were surrounded by green pastures for cows.

High on top of the truck, I was finally unafraid of the cows. But it was night, and I was afraid of bullets that might cry in the darkness and the men who might leap from the side of the road. Mama had told me how one of my aunts died on this very road. She'd been riding on a Fuso like ours when bandits had forced the truck to stop. Mama didn't know why the men had fired their guns or why my aunt had been killed. She only knew that my aunt's body had been sent on to Goma, where there was no one to claim her—no one knew who she was.

Back in Shahalia, I'd learned to hide in the dark, under blankets or branches. But sitting on the back of a Fuso truck was like sitting on top of a hill. There was nowhere to hide. We pressed our bodies together and prayed for morning to come.

Chapter 24

We arrived with the light of the morning. "God be praised," the passengers around me whispered as our truck pulled to a stop. I was packed between shoulders, and I couldn't see the world below us. In the sky, there were ropes everywhere, hanging from wooden poles and snaking between the tops of houses like vines.

"What are those ropes for?" I asked Mama.

"They are not ropes; they're wires," she said as she tried to explain electricity to me. I didn't understand, but there was no more time for asking questions. Passengers were starting to climb off the Fuso. One of the men took me in his arms and carried me to the edge of the truck. He called to the men below. Hands grabbed me and lowered me to the ground. I was happy to feel the earth, solid beneath me again. The world stopped spinning, and I blinked my eyes, trying to clear the dust and the dizziness from the journey.

Behind the truck, I could see a long line of strong men, shouting and hoisting bags. Beyond them, the street was filled with more people than I had ever seen in my life. Skinny people, big people, and people with their skin tinged red. I was fascinated by the sight of all these different people. Maybe there was a place for me here.

Satisfied to have arrived in Goma, I took a deep breath. The smell of smoke filled my nostrils and choked my throat. It wasn't like the smoke from our fires in Shahalia—this smoke was thick and dark, and it was pouring out of our truck. I tried to crawl away from the smoke, but as soon as my hands touched the ground, they slid through filthy black mud. I pulled my hands back in surprise. The mud was oozing with oil.

This was the dirtiest place I had ever seen. Floating in the mud were paper wrappers and used plastic bags. There was nowhere clean to rest. My nose was too close to the ground. I could smell everything—the smoke and the mud and the garbage, and the women cooking food by the side of the road. The mix of smells twisted my stomach.

We waited until my uncle finished his work on the truck. He motioned for us to follow him into the busy street. As much as I disliked the oily mud where I was sitting, I wasn't sure that I wanted to move. There were people, cars, and motorcycles everywhere.

Mama was watching me carefully. "You crawl in front, I'll follow behind," she said. She had Soleil tied to her back, our bundle on her head, and my two thatch mats under her arms. There was no way Mama could carry me.

I started to crawl, following my uncle. Rocks dug into my legs and my hands. I moved to one side and the other, trying to find a path where there were no rocks. But pointy grey rocks seemed to be growing out of the dirt in every direction.

On the sides of the road, I could see walls, and even those walls were built from pointy grey rocks piled one on top of another. Behind the walls, I saw houses and shops built out of flat boards of wood and spiky tin roofs. Everything looked so sharp.

Soon, we arrived at my uncle's house. It was the first time I remember meeting Ma Mukubwa. She was my mother's older sister, but her face was young and shiny, like a person who no longer worked in the fields. Ma Mukubwa brought a basin of water, and we washed our hands. The black oily mud had soaked between my fingers and under my nails, so I scrubbed until my hands were clean.

I could smell the food on a small table nearby. I was hungry, but before we even prayed for the food Mama announced, "I'm going to take Argentine to the Centre Pour Handicapés."

Ma Mukubwa looked nervous. "Really? Are you sure? But you don't have any money. What if they don't let you in?"

Mama nodded quickly, as though she had already had this conversation before and didn't want to have it again. "We'll find someone to help us," she dismissed.

We gathered around the food to eat. After we finished, I gave Ma Mukubwa one of the thatch mats I had woven. Then Mama spoke.

"Tie some cloth on your hands and knees. The roads here are rocky," she said, and I looked up in surprise.

"We're not sleeping here?" I asked, but Mama was already out the door with Soleil on her back and our bundle on her head. I scrambled behind her.

"Where are we going?"

"We're going to see Pastor Amani," Mama explained as she headed down the street in the afternoon sun. She waited for me to catch up and gestured forward. I didn't understand why we couldn't stay with my uncle and aunt for the night.

I picked my way cautiously through the rocky road, hoping that Pastor Amani's church was somewhere nearby. I checked the sides of the road for a placard reading Church Mahanaime, but all I could see were feet and rocks in every direction. As I made my way forward, I noticed a well-dressed woman in the street ahead of me. My eyes caught on her painted nails. Even the woman's toenails were painted. They shone bright red against the mud in the road. I'd never seen my mother's nails painted. *This must be what women in Goma look like,* I thought.

As I studied the painted woman, she started to shout. "Demayi! Demayi!" she called to someone behind me as she ran by. When I turned my head in curiosity, I was shocked to find this unfamiliar woman throwing her arms around Mama. "What are you doing in Goma?" the painted woman demanded.

Mama pulled back and explained, "I've come with my daughter."

The painted woman turned to look at me. "This is your daughter?" she asked, stepping back and sucking in air. "This is your child?"

"Yego," Mama affirmed.

The woman shook her head fiercely. "But Demayi! What are you doing? How could you bring this girl here? She'll be crushed!"

My legs started to shake. It was true that there were a lot of people on this road. It was like market day, except even more crowded. I had been so busy concentrating on the rocks in the road, and thinking about Pastor Amani's church, that I hadn't noticed all the dangers swirling around me. Now I could see the wooden wheels of overloaded chukudus ready to crush me.

Before Mama could answer, something happened that I never expected. This woman, with her fancy clothes and bright red nails, walked over to me and dropped to her knees in the filthy road. "Climb on my back. I'll take you as far as I can," she offered.

Who was this woman? I knew I was dirty, coated with mud. I was the type of person that people with fancy clothes pass without greeting. Even back in Shahalia, there had been adults who refused to shake my hand. My own cousin didn't want to share food with me. But here was this woman kneeling in the dirt in front of me. I couldn't understand, but I climbed on her back and clung to her shoulders. The painted woman grabbed my dirty legs and wrapped them around her stomach. She covered me with her kitenge, like I was her child.

We walked and walked. Mama and the painted woman took big steps, moving much faster than I could have crawled. At last, we saw a sign for Church Mahanaime, and Mama's tired face lit up. "That's him! That's Pastor Amani," she said, pointing toward a man who was sitting on a rock, his bald head shining in the late afternoon sun. He waved his hand and called us over. That's when I saw his face. It was as generous as I had remembered. This was Pastor Amani.

When he looked at us, Pastor Amani seemed more surprised by the painted woman than by Mama or me. "Who is this woman?" Pastor Amani asked, eyeing her clothing.

"We knew each other years ago in Masisi," Mama explained as her voice trailed off. This woman did not look like someone who'd ever lived in the hills of Masisi.

Pastor Amani looked at the painted woman, then spoke. "You've done a good thing," he said to her quietly.

And then, right there by the side of the road, Pastor Amani asked the woman to kneel. I couldn't believe it. This woman with her fancy clothes and painted nails was kneeling in the street again. "We'll pray God's blessing upon you for what you have done," Pastor Amani said, and tears rolled down the woman's face.

After the prayer, we thanked the painted woman, and she walked off. I still didn't understand who this woman was, or why Pastor Amani had been so surprised to see her with us. I didn't know the things that had been said about her back in Masisi. I didn't know where she got her money or her painted nails. I only knew that this woman had carried me like I was her child, and that was all I needed to know.

Chapter 25

At Pastor Amani's church, they were holding a prayer retreat. We slept at the church that night, and the next day the whole congregation prayed for us. Afterward, Pastor Amani offered to take us to his house nearby, and Mama accepted his offer. I was anxious to continue our journey to the Centre, but I had to admit that I was hungry and tired. Maybe going to Pastor Amani's house first was a good idea.

When we set out on the road, it seemed even more rocky than it had the day before. As soon as I touched the road with my hands, I jumped back in surprise. It was midday, and the rocks were so hot that they burned my skin. I scooted toward a sandy patch by the side of the road, but even the sand was so hot that it burned my hands. I looked around for a tree where I could find shade, but there were no trees in this neighborhood. There were only rock walls, and houses made from wood slats, painted brown with motor oil to keep out the bugs.

Thankfully, Pastor Amani's house was nearby. As soon as we arrived, Pastor Amani's wife welcomed us generously. She thanked me for the woven mat that I gave her. "Argentine, you are welcome here anytime," she said.

I could see that there were already many children in this small house, but Mama Pastor looked unconcerned. She motioned for the children to move closer together to make room for us.

After food and a night of rest, Mama said it was time to go to the Centre. I felt relieved. We'd come through the swamp and the banana stalks and the fiery hot road. I was anxious to finish our journey.

We left in the morning so that the road wouldn't be so hot. On the side of the road, there were women sitting at low wooden tables next to pyramids of tomatoes and onions. Other women were roasting corn and squatting beside wide-mouthed pots of oil, frying mandazi. I'd never seen anyone cooking by the side of the road before.

I was so excited to see the corn and mandazis being cooked that I didn't realize how we must have looked. We'd been traveling for a long time. I was limping and hobbling on my hands and knees through the crowded streets of Goma. My mother was carrying Soleil and our bundle of things, and she was growing exhausted.

A woman called out to us from the side of the road. "Here, take this," she said, offering a roasted cob of corn. Another woman, at a table nearby, stretched out her hand with a plastic bag of blue, powdery soap. Mama accepted the offerings with both hands.

I didn't know how desperate we looked—how desperate we were. But Mama knew. She lowered her head and thanked everyone. That was the only thing she had left to give: her thanks.

"Mungu akubariki," she said. "God bless you."

From the moment we'd left Shahalia, Mama had been throwing us on the mercy of others. Ruberiti, Rupyisi, and Ndahimana. Majinaa. My uncle on the Fuso and my aunt with her face still young. The woman with the painted nails. Pastor Amani and his wife. We had passed through the hands of so many people. And now in the rocky streets of Goma, strangers were handing us corn and blue, powdery soap.

When we arrived at the corner, Mama started talking to people in the street, explaining that we wanted to go to the Centre Pour Handicapés and asking where we might find the right bus. She was speaking Swahili, even though back in Shahalia we spoke Kinyarwanda. I'd learned Swahili from some of the songs that Safari had taught us and from some of the visitors who came to our house. But now, here in Goma, Swahili was loud and difficult to understand.

The people in the street pointed us toward minibuses parked by the side of the road. Boys were hanging out the open doors of the buses, banging on the roofs, and calling out unfamiliar names. We climbed onto a crowded bus. It was hot and sticky with the smell of sweat. The bus traveled forward. Eventually, we jerked to a stop, and Mama and I climbed off the bus.

As we climbed off the bus, Mama said something to the boy at the door, and he pointed us down the street. Mama started walking, and I crawled eagerly beside her. We passed through a gate and into a crowded, walled-off compound. This was the Centre. We had arrived. I was thrilled. I pulled back my shoulders and started looking around. There were people everywhere. They were standing in lines, sitting on chairs, and squatting.

I searched for other girls like me—the ones Mama had told me about. We were surrounded by many children, but none of them had legs like mine. Instead, they had dry faces, orange-white hair, and big stomachs. They reminded me of the children I'd seen arrive in Shahalia—the ones who begged for something to eat.

Frantically I scanned the crowds looking for the doctors in white. I couldn't find a single doctor. *Where are we?* I wanted to ask. This was not the place of my dreams.

As I stared into the throngs of tired women and hungry children, my eyes fell on a long, narrow face. "Mama, we know her!" I exclaimed, pointing my head toward the woman. Mama squinted for a moment. She looked so tired that I wasn't sure if she could see anything. But after a moment, a flash of recognition crossed Mama's face, and she smiled.

"Yes! It's Nyirarugendo!" Mama said.

It had been years since we had seen this woman's face, but I still remembered her from Shahalia. She'd sung in the choir with Mama, and one year her belly had swollen so round that I thought she would pop. She'd given birth to triplets and left for Goma in hopes of finding food for her three babies. Now, here she was.

Mama raced over to Nyirarugendo. The women embraced. There was nodding and laughter, but, after some time, Mama returned with her shoulders slumped.

"This isn't the Centre Pour Handicapés," Mama admitted. "It's a place that feeds hungry children."

"But why? Why did the bus driver bring us here?" I sputtered. When I looked down at my own clothes, I began to understand. This was a place for needy people. I thought of the women by the side of the road, offering us cobs of corn and blue, powdery soap. "God help you," they'd whispered sympathetically. Even Nyirarugendo had looked sorry for us. This was a place for needy people, and we were people who needed help.

Mama could hardly stand on her feet anymore, but she tried to smile. "Let's not cut hope," she said as she stumbled toward a rock to sit on.

Nyirarugendo had told Mama that a mzungu—a white woman—would be arriving at the feeding center soon. "She's very kind. Maybe she'll help you." Nyirarugendo had explained.

We sat there and waited. I'd never seen a mzungu before. I'd heard they did terrible things, but I tried not to cut hope. Across the compound, in an open-air pavilion, women were cooking in giant black pots. They ladled brown porridge into plastic mugs.

Soon, a long, shiny white vehicle arrived, and a woman with white skin climbed out. The crowds pressed tight around her, and her white blouse and shiny hair vanished behind a wall of people. Everyone was calling out their needs to this woman, and we were far away. She'd never be able to see us, and there was no way to get closer. There were so many people and so many needs, and we were villagers lost in the crowds. Soon, the woman climbed in the shiny white vehicle and left again. She never even saw us.

I turned to look at Mama. She was still sitting on a rock, her body folded over her stomach. She was sick. We were never going to make it to the Centre now. I thought of my father's words. "You might as well be hanging yourself," he had told Mama. And now Mama was sick and exhausted. I was nothing but a burden. My father was right. Mama should have stayed home and taken care of her other children.

Just as I was starting to despair, Nyirarugendo returned, clucking softly. "I'll take you home with me," she said as she led us back into the crowded road.

Chapter 26

Nyirarugendo's house was smaller than Pastor Amani's house. She was a person in need of help—like us. She'd left Shahalia because she couldn't find a way to feed her triplets in the village. In Goma, we'd found her standing in line for porridge at a feeding center. And now, here we were, collapsed on Nyirarugendo's floor. I didn't even have a thatch mat to give her.

Nyirarugendo didn't seem worried about what we could give her. Instead, she brought medicine for Mama and told us to rest. In the morning, I awoke to Nyirarugendo wondering aloud what Mama could eat. Nyirarugendo offered sweet potatoes, mboga buchungu, and ibiteri. Every day, Nyirarugendo tried to find something that Mama could eat.

As the days passed, Mama began to grow stronger. Eventually, she said she was ready to continue our journey. "We'll go to the Centre now," she said, her voice still sounding faint.

"Really? But you have no money. What if the doctors don't let you in?" Nyirarugendo asked softly.

Mama tied Soleil onto her back and straightened her shoulders. She must have been thinking about our first journey to the Centre, when I was only two years old—the journey I couldn't even remember. "Come back with money next time," the doctors had said. What kind of faith did my mother have? What kind of faith would carry us back to the Centre—empty-handed again?

Mama straightened her shoulders. "God will help us," she told Nyirarugendo.

I tied fabric on my knees and hands, in preparation for the hot, rocky road. After saying goodbye to Nyirarugendo, we headed back toward the main road, but we were moving slowly now. By the time we reached the main road, the sun was setting, and I was losing hope. These were the hours when people walked home from the market, and children ran out to greet their parents. Even if we made it to the Centre Pour Handicapés now, it would be too late in the day, and we would be arriving muddy and empty-handed. I understood now. This was a city already full of people who needed help. There was no place for us here.

I tried to continue crawling, but now I was afraid of everything. I was afraid of the motorcycles buzzing by and the heavy carts and the cars. If only I had a chukudu and someone to push me. I scanned the road, but every wooden scooter was already overflowing with heavy sacks.

That's when I noticed something strange rolling toward us. There was a beautiful woman sitting on top of a device that I had never seen before. It looked like a bicycle with three oversized wheels. The woman perched on top was pedaling her arms instead of her legs. Behind her, boys were helping to push. The device looked sturdy and strong, and the woman was steering herself.

I understood immediately that this was a device built for someone like me. It was the most wonderful thing I had ever seen.

The woman stopped. She had a serious face, but when she saw me, she smiled broadly and turned to Mama. "You look like guests here. Where are you from?"

"Masisi," Mama answered.

The woman clicked her tongue. "And where are you going?"

"We want to go to the Centre Pour Handicapés," Mama explained, "but we are lost, and we have no money."

The woman was already shaking her head. "It's too late. I can't take you to the Centre tonight. Try to find somewhere to sleep, and I'll take you tomorrow," she suggested.

My hope sank. How would we ever find somewhere to sleep? It was too late to crawl all the way back to Nyirarugendo's house.

I could feel the woman looking at me. I lowered my head. The fabric had slipped down from my knees. My skin was scrapped and bloody. "This child—she can't crawl any further," the woman murmured. "I suppose—let's see—maybe she can come with me," the woman continued, nodding toward a place on her tricycle where I could sit.

Mama quickly agreed. I would go home with this woman, and Mama and Soleil would find somewhere else to sleep. We'd meet again in the morning.

It happened so easily. Without even thinking, Mama and I were separated.

I climbed onto the woman's tricycle and waved goodbye to my mother and Soleil. I knew this woman on the tricycle would take good care of me. I could see her bent legs peeking out from under her kikwembe. Her legs were disabled. I had finally found someone like me. Even her name filled me with confidence. Her name was Mamí.

Mamí peddled her hands, and we rolled forward. "This is my kinga," she explained as I held on to the sides of the metal frame. I knew what kinga meant. It meant bicycle in Swahili, and I had seen bicycles before. But this was a type of kinga I had never seen. In the back there was a platform, loaded with

Fanta bottles in a plastic crate. As we made our way through the bumpy street, the bottles rattled, and Mamí saw me looking at them. "That is my work," she told me. "I carry bottles across the border to Rwanda every day."

Each explanation only invited more questions from me. "Where is Rwanda? How far do you travel?" I asked. My mother was gone, and there was no one to remind me to circle my tongue.

We stopped in front of a small wooden house with a shop attached to the side. The door of the shop was open. On the wooden shelves I saw bottles of water, jugs of oil, and plastic bags filled with salt and blue, powdery soap. "That is my shop," Mamí said. Her words thrilled my heart. Mamí, a woman like me, had her own shop. A little boy ran out of the house, jumping with excitement.

"Who is that?" I asked.

"He is my child."

All my life I had created dolls for myself, dolls out of purple banana buds, dolls out of cloth, and dolls out of avocado seeds. But I thought that's all I would ever have. I visited my neighbors and held their newborn babies close to my heart. I'd even held Nyirarugendo's three babies when they were first born in our village.

Now, looking at this child jumping up and down before Mamí, a new thought arrived in my head. One day I could be like Mamí. I could have a kinga, and a shop, and I could even have a child of my own.

Mamí climbed down from her kinga, and I could barely believe my eyes. She lowered herself to the ground and crawled like me. The mist lifted from the road that day. I could see a future for myself. There were people like me in this world.

Chapter 27

When I awoke the next morning, all my fears were finished, and I was eager to continue our journey. Mamí and I climbed back onto her kinga. She called for two boys to push us, and we rolled through the street, toward the intersection where we would meet Mama.

I loved being off the ground where my hands wouldn't get dirty. Mamí had given me water to bathe the previous night, and I was going to arrive at the Centre Pour Handicapés looking clean and fresh, like a person of meaning.

Pow! There was an explosion. Our kinga jerked to a stop. I whipped my head around searching for a place to hide, but there was nowhere to hide on top of the kinga.

That's when I noticed that no one else looked scared. People were still walking calmly in the street. Women were selling tomatoes. Mamí must have seen the frantic expression on my face. "Don't be afraid. It's only our tire," she explained. She called to the boys, and they tried to push our kinga again. Their thin arms grew tight, but the kinga was sitting lopsided in the street, and we barely moved.

"We're too heavy," Mamí said. "You have to get down." I crawled off the kinga, and the boys pushed again. The kinga limped forward. Mamí turned back to me. "Wait over there, by the side of the road. I'm going to fix the kinga, and I'll come back for you soon."

I didn't want to be left by the side of the road. I didn't want to be left there any more than I wanted to be left under banana stalks or on top of a hill called Gapfura. But I knew Mamí had to go, and I was sure that she would come back for me soon.

"Stay there. Don't move until I return," Mamí warned as the boys pushed the kinga slowly away.

After they left, I sat by the side of the road, afraid to move. In front of me was an intersection with shouting and honking. A man in a blue uniform stood in the center of the intersection blowing a whistle. He looked over at me. I turned away.

I sat there for a long time. The sun rose sharp in the sky, and I felt hot—hotter than I'd ever been in Shahalia. There were no banana stalks and no trees, no shade at all. Boys walked by clinking bottles of Fanta. I was so thirsty. I couldn't stop thinking about our spring in Shahalia where fresh water flowed from the rocks. In Goma, there were so many rocks, but there was no water at all. My stomach rumbled. It had been a long time since we ate.

I thought about Mama. I knew she was standing with Soleil at our meeting spot waiting for Mamí and me to arrive.

The man in the blue uniform walked toward me. "You can't stay here much longer," he said in Swahili. I stared back at him. He nodded at the darkening sky. "Where are you trying to go?" he continued.

I understood the man's Swahili, but I wasn't sure whether I should talk to him. His blue uniform made me nervous. In Shahalia, when men in uniforms walked down our footpath, parents called their children inside and shut their doors. No one wanted to get caught by a soldier. Who knew what they might demand?

This man didn't have a gun, but he looked official. His uniform and his whistle made me nervous. I tried swirling my tongue in my mouth, but I couldn't even do that. My mouth was too dry.

"Where are you going?" the man repeated.

"Centre Pour Handicapés." I finally whispered.

The man glanced through the street, then looked back at me skeptically. Before I knew what was happening, he was motioning to a car. He talked to the driver and opened the back door of the car.

"Get in," the man in the blue uniform said.

I peered at the open door. I'd never ridden in a car before, and I couldn't even see who was driving. I looked back at the place where I had been sitting—the place where Mamí had left me. "Don't move," she had said, just like Mama always said.

I knew I should stay where I was, but the man with the blue uniform was pushing me forward.

"Get in. This car will take you to the Centre Pour Handicapés," he urged.

Maybe the man was right. I was a person in need of help. I couldn't say no. I climbed into the back of the car.

Quickly, the man with the blue uniform slammed the door shut, and the car swerved into the moving traffic. My stomach lurched. I spun my head, searching for the intersection where I had been sitting, but it was already gone. I was lost.

Chapter 28

It wasn't long before the car stopped. "That is the Centre Pour Handicapés," the driver said as he opened the door. "Knock on that gate over there."

I slid out of the vehicle, and the man drove away, leaving me huddled by the side of the road. I couldn't believe it. I had arrived at the place of my dreams. All I had to do was knock on this gate.

Instead of moving, I stared at the gate. It was blue—tall and strong—nothing like the wobbly wooden doors of Shahalia. I knew I would be safe inside a place like this. But I couldn't bring myself to crawl any closer. The more I looked at that gate, the more nervous I became. It was wide enough for cars to drive through. It didn't look like a gate that would open for someone small like me.

I thought of the way everyone kept sucking their teeth when Mama said she was taking me to the Centre. "But you don't have any money! Are you sure they will let you in?" people had asked.

I looked at my hands. They were dirty. I rubbed my fingers against my shorts, trying to clean them, but my shorts were dirty too. I couldn't knock on this gate now. I'd be arriving empty-handed, without even my mother beside me. She was probably still waiting for me at that intersection, the place where we were supposed to meet in the morning.

As soon as I thought of Mama, I knew I had to go back. I couldn't go forward without Mama. I couldn't do anything without Mama. She was my legs. She was my life. I took one more look at the shiny gate—the place of my dreams—then turned away. I had to find Mama.

I started to crawl back down the street, away from the Centre. Soon, I saw a woman carrying a bundle on her head and a child on her back. It was Mama! She'd found me! I scrambled forward, eager to throw myself into Mama's arms, but as I approached, I saw it wasn't Mama at all. It was a woman shaking her head sympathetically as she walked by.

I scanned the road in front of me again. There were people, bicycles, chukudus, wooden carts, and motorcycles, all pushing for space, and I could no longer tell if I was moving in the right direction. I thought of Mamí. Her kinga would be fixed now. She must have gone back looking for me. I was lost, and no one in the whole world knew where I was.

Up ahead I saw a kinga. I was sure it was Mamí. She had found me. She would take me to my mother. But as the kinga grew closer, I could see it wasn't Mamí driving the kinga. It was an old man.

"Ehh? What are you doing?" the man on the kinga demanded.

"I'm looking for my mother," I explained.

He looked doubtfully at the darkening street. "Do you know where she is?"

I twisted my head, trying to recognize the way forward, but all I could see were legs and feet in every direction. The man looked at my face and let out a low whistle. "Listen, you won't find her tonight," he said.

I stared at the old man in his kinga. He was muttering to himself now. "I can't leave you here..." he seemed to be saying. After a moment, his face brightened. "Climb on my kinga. I know a place I can take you," he said.

I trusted this man. He was driving a kinga like Mamí, and I could tell he had a disability like us. Besides, I knew I couldn't crawl anymore.

I climbed on the kinga and held tight to the metal frame. The man pedaled his hands, and I watched the faces passing by, still hoping that I might find Mama.

We traveled on that kinga until the road emptied out, and we arrived in a quiet neighborhood with rock walls so tall that I could see nothing behind. I began to wonder where this man was taking me. I should have stayed at the Centre. My mother could have found me there. With each turn, I was only becoming more lost.

The old man stopped his kinga on the side of an empty street. He pointed at a red gate ahead and told me to climb down from his kinga. I lowered myself onto the street, waiting for the man to join me. "Knock on that gate. But don't tell anyone I brought you here," he whispered firmly, and before I could say anything, the old man and his kinga had disappeared.

This gate was as sturdy and tall as the gate at the Centre Pour Handicapés, except now the road was empty, and I was alone. Evening was coming. It was everything I had feared. It was worse than hiding in the banana stalks. At least in Shahalia, I had known which direction was home. But now I had no home—nowhere to go back to. Shahalia no longer existed in my head. The only thing that was real was Mama, and I had lost her.

Chapter 29

I threw myself on God's mercy and knocked on the bottom of the gate. A man in a uniform opened a narrow door inside the gate. Behind him I could see a world of green. There were trees and flowers, and everything shone clean and fresh. My attention turned back to the man at the gate. He was squinting at the empty road and searching for who had knocked. I was so small and low to the ground that he didn't even see me. I coughed, and he lowered his gaze.

"Weye. Umetoka wapi?" he asked. "You? Where have you come from?"

"Nimetoka Masisi," I answered. "I've come from Masisi." I was speaking softly, stumbling over my words in Swahili.

The man's face twitched. "Masisi? But who brought you all the way here?"

"A man in a kinga..." I started to answer, until I remembered the man's stern warning. I closed my mouth and circled my tongue, trying to find the right words.

"What was the man's name?" the guard demanded.

"I don't know—I am looking for my mother—I am lost," I explained desperately.

The man's face twitched again. "Wait here," he said, walking away and leaving the gate open a crack.

I sat in front of the red gate, waiting for the guard to return. My thoughts swirled. Maybe, if I had arrived earlier in the day, they would have let me in. But now it was late. Darkness was coming. Who would open their door to a visitor at this time of day? Where was I going to spend the night? I couldn't stay in the street. What if a dog attacked? What if a man came and did terrible things?

There was only one solution. I needed God to save me just like he saved Mama in the river in Mweso. I started to pray.

A woman pulled open the door. She was round, with a pleated skirt that was so long it covered her feet. Her skin glowed whiter than anyone I had ever seen. I shrank back. In Shahalia, I'd heard that white people eat children. "Don't stay out too late or the white people will eat you," they'd say. It was like telling children to drink the dew off the mahole leaves. That dew had never stopped my brothers from peeing at night, and I didn't think that white people really ate children. But I couldn't be sure. I'd never met a mzungu before.

The woman smiled. A gold tooth sparkled in the back of her mouth and soft words in Swahili fell out. I was so happy that this strange woman spoke a language I could understand. She was a person, like me. Her hair was pulled back from her face with a band of cloth. Her eyes were soft and full of kindness.

"I'm Sister Louise," she introduced herself. "Where are you from?"

When I answered, she looked surprised. "Masisi?! I am so sorry," she whispered gently. Then she called for the guard to open the gate. "You'll sleep here with us tonight. In the morning, we'll find your mother."

I let out all the air I had been holding inside my chest. I could breathe again. The dogs wouldn't get me. The terrible men wouldn't come. I had a safe place to sleep. As I crawled through the gate, I was welcomed by the smell of flowers. The grass tickled my skin. Ever since we arrived in Goma, my knees had been scraped raw by the rocks, but here the ground was soft and welcoming. There were no zooming motorcycles or shouting people. Sister Louise started to walk, her pleated skirt swishing. She led me into one of the buildings.

Inside, I found myself in a room with a wooden bed. I'd never seen such a tall bed before. In Shahalia, we slept on mats laid on the ground or suspended between sticks. This bed was too tall. I couldn't climb up. I planted my hands onto the smooth cement floor and looked pleadingly at Sister Louise.

After a few minutes, she seemed to understand. She pulled the mattress onto the cement floor, and I touched it gingerly. It was so soft. Sister Louise left the room and returned with another woman. They brought blankets and a plate of fish in a red sauce. The smell delighted me. I took a bite. It was delicious. Later, Sister Louise returned. She asked if I was ready to sleep, and, when I said yes, she reached out toward the wall.

"It will be very dark," she warned. I nodded, but I didn't understand. I knew only candles and kerosene lamps, and I didn't understand why she was reaching toward the wall.

When Sister Louise touched the wall, darkness swallowed the room. "Return the light!" I cried, and the room filled with brightness again.

"I'll leave the light on," Sister Louise said gently as she closed the door.

After Sister Louise left, I lay on the foam mattress and stared above me. The light was too bright. It reminded me of those terrible flashlights—the light that spun through our house and burned our eyes when the attackers came. I tried to squeeze my eyes shut, but my heart continued to pound. It was too quiet. I could hear my own breath, quick and shallow. I had never slept in a room by myself. I missed the rhythmic sound of my brothers breathing and the warmth of their bodies. I missed the smell of Mama's skin.

I lay on that mattress all night with my body tense against the soft foam. I closed my eyes, but I never slept.

When the morning light filtered through the window, I heard footsteps outside. A woman pushed open the door. "Sister Louise sent me," she said.

This woman had dark skin like me. I followed her to a room where she twisted a metal tap. Water spilled out. "This is how we fetch water here," she explained, and I stared at the water trying to imagine what spring it had come from. Gingerly, I reached out a hand. The water was too cold, but I washed with it anyway, and hurried outside, eager for the warmth of the sun.

Outside, I fixed my eyes on the red gate waiting for Mama to enter. I knew she would come for me, like a mother bird returns for her babies.

Except, as I sat in Sister Louise's compound looking at the red gate, I realized that I was sitting behind a wall. Mama would never find me here. I rushed out the gate and sat by the side of the road where Mama could see me.

Many people walked by, but Mama didn't come. When the sun rose high in the sky, Sister Louise peeked outside the gate and motioned for me to come back inside. I crawled sadly back through the gate. Sister Louise looked at me softly. "Are you sure that your mother is coming for you?"

I straightened my neck, pulling away. What was she saying? What kind of mother wouldn't look for her child? My mother had carried me all the way from Shahalia to Goma. She wouldn't abandon me now.

"My mother is looking for me," I insisted.

"Don't worry, we'll find her then," Sister Louise reassured.

As we sat together, Sister Louise continued talking. I didn't understand everything she was saying, but I heard one thing.

She said that if my mother didn't arrive soon, they would put me on the radio to make an announcement.

I dug my fingers into the grass underneath me. *A radio?* How would they put my voice on a radio? In my mind, there was no end to the astonishing things that Sister Louise might do. She was a miracle. Her whole existence was an astonishment to me, with her blue eyes and white skin and gold tooth that sparkled. She could make water pour out of walls. She could make light in the darkness. And now she was going to put me on the radio.

I couldn't stop my mind from tumbling forward in terror. I had seen the tall poles with wires strung between them. Mama had tried to explain electricity to me. I didn't understand how radios worked, and I didn't understand how electricity worked, but the two were linked in my mind. I could see myself being raised to the top of a pole to make an announcement. I sat on the grass and prayed fervently that God would save me from this terrible fate.

Just then the red gate swung open. A wheel came through the gate. And a kinga rolled in. It was Mamí in her kinga, the tire now fixed. My eyes scrambled past Mamí to the woman standing beside her. Her feet were muddy from the road. And her kikwembe was tied loosely around her waist. There was a child on her back and a bundle on her head. It was Mama! She looked exhausted. But Mama had found me.

Mama ran over and wrapped me in her arms. Behind my mother, Sister Louise was watching. She looked at my mother's wet face and the way we clung to each other.

"Argentine, you were right. Your mother loves you very much," she said.

In the time that followed, Sister Louise had many questions for Mama. She wanted to know if we had really come from the hills of Masisi. As Mama spoke, Sister Louise's face furrowed into a mixture of surprise and disbelief. Mama tried to explain what it was like to live in Masisi. She talked about hiding me under banana leaves and about bullets that cried in the night. She talked about Rupyisi and Ruberiti and Ndahimana pushing me on a chukudu, and about how she didn't know if we'd ever make it to the Centre Pour Handicapés.

"Don't you have any family in Goma?" Sister Louise asked.

"We have no one," Mama answered.

I looked at Mama in surprise. She hadn't said anything about Ma Mukubwa. How had she forgotten about her own sister? I started to open my mouth, but Mama arched her eyebrows at me, drawing lines into her smooth forehead. I clamped my mouth shut.

"What about your husband? Where is he?" Sister Louise continued with her questions.

"We have no one," Mama repeated firmly, her eyes still fixed on me. I circled my tongue. I was beginning to understand what Mama meant. What good would it do to mention my father or my brothers back in Mweso? They couldn't help us now. We had no one who could help us—no one except this stout woman.

In the gap that Mama created, Sister Louise spoke. "Don't worry. I'll take you to the Centre myself," she promised.

There it was. We were going to the Centre, and this time I wouldn't arrive alone.

Sister Louise fetched a bicycle that was leaning nearby. She pulled up her long skirt as she climbed onto the bicycle. Then she asked Mamí to carry me in her kinga again. Mamí agreed. Soon the red gate opened, and we were making our way down the road—Sister Louise riding a bicycle, Mamí and I in the kinga, and Mama and Soleil walking beside us. I was pleased to be riding on Mamí's kinga again, but this time I didn't let my eyes leave Mama. After a few minutes, Sister Louise stopped her bicycle and waited for us. When we came close, she whispered another promise.

"If the doctors at the Centre agree to take you, I'll pay for the treatment myself."

Mama and I looked at each other. It was like the river in Mweso. We were saved—pulled from the water. We'd seen death and survived. We were going to arrive at the Centre, and we were no longer arriving empty-handed. I thought of all the people who had said, "Are you sure? But you don't have any money."

"God will help us," Mama had answered. And now, here was Sister Louise, offering to help us. Our tears had turned to joy, and nothing could stop us now.

Chapter 30

From the moment we entered that gate, I knew I'd found the place of my dreams. The buildings were painted white with blue trim. Cement walkways led to every doorway. People were walking on crutches and leaning on canes and sitting in chairs with wheels. To live your life without seeing anyone like you is to suffer. *Why is it me? Why only me?* I had wondered all my life. But now I could see that it wasn't only me. I had found the place where I belonged.

At the Centre, everyone knew Sister Louise and her bicycle. People peeked out of their offices, peered at me, and said, "So this is Sister Louise's child. You're very lucky." And I felt lucky. I saw the doctors in white. They were there talking to Sister Louise. I waited for them to circle around me and look at my legs just as I had dreamed.

But instead, the doctors spoke quietly to Sister Louise. They nodded and waved goodbye.

"They're going to schedule a consultation for you," Sister Louise explained. When she saw my confused expression, she continued, "It's an appointment where they will look at your legs and decide if they can help you."

My heart knocked on my chest. What did she mean? *If...if they can help me?* These were the people from my dream. They were wearing white. They were the doctors. Of course, they could help me. They were the only ones in the world who could help me. I wanted to tell them that, but they were already gone, and a woman was leading us out of the Centre, back through the compound with its easy walkways. The woman led us out of the gate and into the dirty streets of Goma. The metal clanked behind us. We'd come all this way, and now we were leaving again.

The woman from the Centre led us across the street and into a neighborhood where the wooden houses were stuck together in long rows. The sharp bite of a pit latrine filled my nose. I picked my way carefully through the filthy path and followed the woman into a house. There were two rooms lined with beds. "This is the maison de passage—the guest house. You can sleep here," the woman said. She left without waiting for questions.

Sister Louise stood in the maison de passage with us and looked sadly around at the cramped room. "The doctors will send for you soon," she promised as she moved toward the door. I didn't want Sister Louise to leave. I loved her gentle voice and the way her back tooth sparkled with every word.

After Sister Louise left, we collapsed onto a narrow bed. We slept there that night, wondering what it meant to be in this place. The beds were lined so close to each other that we could touch the strangers sleeping next to us. I was ashamed of my body. How could I change clothes in this place where strangers would see my skinny, curled-up legs and my crooked back? The pit latrine outside was covered in waste. If I crawled in there, I knew I'd return filthy. I wondered how many days I could avoid that place. I tried to keep everything inside me, even my doubts.

Day after day, I sat in that guest house and looked out the open window, watching for someone in white to arrive. No one came.

"Don't be afraid," a woman at the guest house tried to encourage me. "You're lucky! You have someone to pay for your treatment. They'll call for you soon."

But what if Sister Louise never came back? What if she decided not to pay for my treatment after all? What if the doctors never called for me? I was desperate to leave this guest house where I couldn't even change my clothes. I wanted to go back to the Centre, with the white buildings and smooth walkways and people like me.

Finally, I could wait no longer. I slipped out the door of the guest house and crawled to the gate of the Centre, where I waited for someone to exit. When the gate opened, I crawled quickly inside. As soon as I arrived, everything changed. I could breathe again. This was where I belonged. I settled onto a patch of grass where no one seemed to notice me. I felt like I had in Shahalia, on market day, watching our path fill with people. Doctors rushed past in their white jackets. To me, everyone wearing white was a doctor.

This is the place I want to be, I thought to myself, as I tried to imagine how I could stay. I had nothing to offer anyone here. My thatch mats were gone. I thought of the way Mama had thanked the women by the side of the road—the ones who gave us cobs of corn and blue soap. I would do what my mother had done. "Mungu akubariki—God bless you," I'd say to everyone who passed.

Some of the people in white looked busy. They didn't raise their eyes when I greeted them. But there were others who smiled and returned my greetings. Some people started to learn my name. "Hi Argentine! Are you doing well?" they called out in Kinyarwanda, or Swahili, or French.

Soon I met the girls my age. Some of them stood on crutches with their legs in metal braces. Others sat in wheelchairs which I had never seen before. I studied those wheelchairs, fascinated. One of the girls was named Charlotte, but everyone called her Shayo. We were almost the same age. "Da Shayo, here comes your twin," people started chuckling when I would arrive.

Shayo had light skin and thoughtful eyes. And she was quiet in all the ways that I was loud. But one day she called me close and explained how her legs had been bent like mine. Now her legs were covered in something white and hard like a rock. Shayo told me it was called plaster.

"Will they cover my legs in plaster too?" I asked hopefully, thinking that I could be like Shayo, but then I remembered the guest house with its filthy latrine and rows of narrow beds—the place where I was stuck. "Why haven't they called for me? What if the doctors say they can't treat me? What if they send me back to Masisi?" I couldn't stop my tumbling questions.

"All you can do is wait," Shayo answered softly.

Waiting was difficult. In the evening, my friends said good-bye and glided into the salle à manger—the room for eating—and I carried myself back down the cement walkways and out of the Centre. The metal gate clanked shut behind me. I picked my way past the pit latrine and into the guest house, where I lay with Mama and Soleil pressed into one bed, and strangers breathing beside us. I thought of the Centre and all the girls like me. I had found the place where I belonged—the place of my dreams—if only they would let me in.

Chapter 31

Weeks passed that way, with me crawling into the Centre during the day and returning to the guest house at night. We waited for something to happen. Sister Louise visited again, bringing us food. "They still haven't called for you?" she asked, with a worried expression on her face.

Then one day, someone came. A boy arrived with a message that the doctors wanted to see me the next day. Mama and I swooped our voices into a cheer that turned into a prayer. That is what it means to have nothing. It means to pray. To pray without ceasing. Every breath turns into a prayer. In that guest house outside of the Centre, we had prayed so many prayers that we couldn't add them all up, and now God was answering our prayers.

We hurried to the Centre the next morning. When we entered the long, white building, it smelled like something unfamiliar. Mama and I were separated. Someone gave me a wheelchair and pushed me into a room. My mother sat outside.

In the room with the chipped paint, a person in white pointed toward a table. More people in white arrived. They circled around me, just like my dream.

"Lie on your back," a white coat instructed, and I lay on my back.

"Wiggle your toes," he said. I concentrated. I stared hard at my toes.

The doctor's gaze shifted from my toes to my calves. "Lift your leg," he said. I sighed in relief. At least I knew how to lift my leg. I was always hoisting my legs around. I sat up and reached forward, picking up my leg with my hands. The doctor shook his head.

"No. Not with your hands. Raise your leg on its own," he said. My leg moved a little.

The doctors in white jackets squinted at me. They wrote on their clipboards, without saying a word. No one smiled.

"Does your back hurt?" a woman asked. My mind scrambled over possible answers. *Yes? No?* Which answer would allow me to stay?

"She'll be like Bunyere," I heard someone say. My mind spun, but I couldn't remember meeting anyone named Bunyere, so I didn't know whether I wanted to be like her or not.

A woman with a white coat pointed at my legs and my back. She shook her head. "This child will not walk," she said in French. I shouldn't have been able to understand her, but I did.

Fear crawled through my body. They couldn't send us home now. Everyone in Shahalia would shake their heads and click their tongues at my mother—at her foolishness in carrying me all the way to the Centre. "Why do you keep carrying that girl of yours?" they'd ask sadly.

A short doctor with glasses spoke. I knew his face. I'd seen him walk by me every day in his white coat while I sat outside in the sun greeting people. "Bonjour," he'd say without looking up. He never smiled.

Now, the short doctor studied me through his glasses. "Argentine," he said softly. My name rolled off his tongue as though he'd known it all along. "Have you talked to the other girls?" he asked. "Have you talked to Shayo? Have you talked to Josephine?"

"Yes, Doctor," I replied, thankful for such an easy question and happy to think of my new friends.

"Did they tell you what the treatment is like?"

"Yes, Doctor."

"Do you understand that it isn't going to be easy?"

"Yes, Doctor."

"Will you be patient?"

"Yes, Doctor," I said, stumbling over my own eagerness. *Of course, I can be patient*, I wanted to shout. *I'll be whatever they want me to be.*

"Write her name down," the doctor with glasses said. "This child will learn to walk."

My heart bloomed. This was the answer to all my prayers.

Later that evening, when I was sitting outside with my new friends, they asked me about the consultation and laughed at my description of the short doctor who didn't smile. "Oh, that is Dr. Hari," they squealed and pounded the table "He will straighten you out for real!"

I was so happy to have arrived at the place of my dreams. We were here, and no one was going to send us home now. But then I looked at my mother, and I remembered what else Dr. Hari had said that morning. After they had finished looking at me, Dr. Hari had called my mother into the room.

"Mama Argentine, if we agree to treat your daughter, you must remain here at the Centre," he'd said, his mouth set in a line. "You can't go back to Masisi."

I thought of it now, as the other girls continued laughing and sharing stories about the different doctors. *What was Dr. Hari asking of Mama?* My brothers were back in Shahalia, waiting for my mother to return. They were waiting like I had waited in the banana stalks, and in the kivumu, and on the hill called Gapfura. "I will come back soon," Mama had promised us all so many times.

But Dr. Hari had told Mama that she couldn't go home. "Your life is here now," he said. "You have to forget what you've left behind."

Chapter 32

That afternoon, Mama Internat, the woman in charge of the dormitory, led us brusquely from room to room. "This is the salle à manger—the room for eating," she said. She led us into another room. There were rows of beds, with the sheets tucked neatly along the sides of each mattress. She pointed at one of the beds. "You'll sleep here," she instructed.

I was finally going to have a bed at the Centre, and I was thrilled. Before I could settle in, Mama Internat strode impatiently out of the dormitory room and through the hallway, motioning for us to follow. I was sitting in a wheelchair. I pushed the metal rims, and the wheels skimmed quickly over the cement floor. Soon, I was out of the room, and down the long hallway. I was free.

That's what the wheelchair felt like to me. Freedom. I'd never been able to carry myself so quickly before. I was high off the ground, and I could finally move as fast as everyone else, even Mama Internat. In Shahalia, I had spent years trailing behind other children. I had crawled on my elbows to keep my hands clean. Now, I had found freedom.

Mama Internat led us into another room. "This is the toilet," she sniffed. "You will not throw leaves in the toilet like a villager. Here, at the Centre, you must be clean." Mama and I ducked our heads and nodded seriously, as though we'd never been clean before—as though Mama had never taught me to sweep our yard until not one stick remained. Ever since we had left Shahalia, we had been at the mercy of strangers, and now we were at the mercy of this sharp woman who thought we couldn't be clean.

Mama Internat led us out of the dormitory and into the fresh air. We passed a kitchen where women were sitting outside on rocks, peeling potatoes. We passed a row of offices where men with polished shoes sat behind desks with binders piled on top. One of the men with polished shoes was standing in a doorway. He smiled and greeted me in a soft voice. He told me he was a social worker. "If you ever need anything, come and see me in my office," he offered. The man's polite voice surprised me. He spoke to me like I was a person of meaning. I didn't know that men could do that—not for someone like me. But even though his voice was soft and polite, I knew I'd never go to that man's office. I wasn't the type of person who belonged in an office.

Across the courtyard was kinesiology—a building that was divided into several rooms. There was an enormous hall with a pointed ceiling. In that room I could see people learning to walk on crutches and climbing up and down stairs. I could see the sweat trickling across patients' faces, and the nervous way they extended their limbs. *Will I have to do that?* I wondered. A knot formed in my stomach. My legs were skinny and bent. My back was curved. How would I ever learn to walk? I grabbed the rims of my wheels and rolled quickly out of the kinesiology room.

In one corner of the Centre, I saw a small building with red, stained-glass windows. We didn't go inside, but I could hear singing. It was the chapel. I knew that was the place for me.

Mama Internat was still issuing warnings as we returned to the dormitory. I tried to listen earnestly, but there was so much to see. I peered into the room next to ours. Two girls were sitting in wheelchairs, but immediately I knew they were nothing like me. They wore waxy kitenge fabric and their hair fell across their shoulders in braids and beads. I reached toward my own head. My hair was short. It had never been braided like that. My T-shirt was loose and faded. My shorts were black. Next to those girls I felt small. When they looked at me, I rolled quickly away.

That night, Mama and Soleil slept in my bed. There was no bed assigned to them. I realized why Dr. Hari had told Mama that she couldn't leave. She was my caregiver. For every sick person at the Centre, there was someone sleeping nearby, usually a mother or sister or cousin. They slept on mats on the cement floor and woke in the morning to fetch water, wash clothes, mop floors and carry the plastic basins that served as chamber pots.

I asked my friend Shayo where her caregiver was, and she nodded toward a skinny girl. "Mdogo wangu," she said. Her little sister.

Shayo explained that their mother had died when they were young. This horrified me. I couldn't imagine how Shayo had survived as a girl who couldn't walk, without even her mother to protect her.

It made me think of my friend Bébé, whose mother had died and whose father had remarried. She had lived in the world with no one to protect her. And that was difficult enough for Bébé—a girl with two good legs and a back strong enough to carry us both. I couldn't imagine how Shayo had survived. Who had carried her to the latrine? How had she arrived at the Centre?

Shayo saw the question on my face. "My father brought me," she explained. That shocked me more than anything else at the Centre—a father who carried his daughter. This was a new world indeed.

Chapter 33

I learned everything from my friends at the Centre. They showed me their plaster-covered legs and told me that soon the doctors would put plaster on my legs too. When the day arrived, I wasn't nervous. I wanted to be like all the other girls. I sat on a table, and Dr. Hari dipped white strips of fabric into a bowl and coated my legs with something that was neither hot nor cold, only soft and wet.

Afterwards, Mama pushed me back toward the dormitory. I was feeling good. I sat outside on the veranda, letting the sun warm my body and waiting for the other girls to return from wherever they had gone. Shayo arrived, and I greeted her happily. Beside her was Francine, a talkative girl who walked on crutches, thudding confidently across the cement.

Francine grinned at me, the gap between her middle teeth showing. "Congratulations Argentine!" she said, nodding toward the plaster on my legs.

I smiled back at her. "Yes! It doesn't even hurt!" I proclaimed proudly.

At my words, Francine burst into laughter. "Wait until Thursday! You'll get your sauce on Thursday!" She choked out the words between giggles. *Sauce?* What was Francine talking about? Who was making a sauce?

Some of the other girls began to hoot, "Her sauce! They're preparing her sauce!"

Bewildered, I looked toward Shayo. Her gentle face had closed into a frown, and the other girls were still laughing.

Even I could tell that this wasn't the right time for questions. I would ask Shayo about it later.

That night, when none of the other girls were listening, I asked Shayo what Francine had been talking about. "What is this sauce?" I whispered, remembering their laughter.

"On Thursday, they'll take you back to kinesiology," Shayo answered.

"But what is this sauce that they'll give me?" I demanded.

Shayo shrugged. "You have to be patient," she said.

Of course, I knew I had to be patient. Ever since I'd arrived at the Centre, everyone had repeated that word back to me. "Utavumilia?" they asked. "Will you be patient?"

"Yes, yes. I'll be patient," I said to Shayo, hurrying her along. "But I don't understand yet. What is this sauce?" I was trying to imagine how the kinesiology room might involve cooking a sauce.

Eventually Shayo had mercy on me. "Argentine, do you know how to make a sauce?"

"The kind of sauce that we eat?" I floundered. Shayo lifted her eyebrows, encouraging me to continue. "You cook sauce with tomato and onion," I answered. Shayo said nothing,

"...and oil and salt," I added.

Shayo prompted me again. "What do you do first?"

I stopped to think. I imagined myself back in Shahalia. "First, you look for firewood," I answered, picturing my brothers ducking beneath trees. "Then, you light a fire," I could feel the smoke burning my eyes. "Next, you put oil in the pan." I heard spitting and sizzling. "Then, you cut tomato and onion and..."

Shayo lifted her hand to stop me. "And only after all of that will you taste your sauce, right?" she prodded.

I stared blankly back at Shayo.

Shayo pointed her chin toward my legs. "They've put on your plaster, but you haven't yet tasted the sauce."

By the time Thursday came, my body was cold with fear. I no longer wanted to taste this sauce or know anything about it. Mama pushed me back to kinesiology, and I waited outside nervously as other patients were wheeled in and out, their plaster-covered legs propped at uncomfortable angles.

When I was called into the room, I pulled myself onto the examination table next to Dr. Hari and several other doctors. They never looked at my face. Instead, they were looking only at my plaster-covered legs.

"Don't move," Dr. Hari said, and a nun with a crucifix dangling from her neck pressed her fingers into my shoulders. From a low shelf, Dr. Hari took out a machine. I looked at it curiously. My eyes followed Dr. Hari as he leaned over to the wall and plugged in a cord. Suddenly, the machine started to scream. Dr. Hari held the machine above my plaster-covered legs.

"We're going to cut this plaster," Dr. Hari said to me.

"But you'll cut my legs!" I squealed.

The nun standing next to me promised that the machine wouldn't cut my legs.

I wasn't sure if I believed her, but her fingers were pressing me down so I couldn't move. I squeezed my eyes shut hoping to disappear. My legs started to vibrate. After a few minutes, the machine fell silent. I thanked God. It was finished. I opened my eyes cautiously and peeked at my legs. They were still covered in plaster. There was only one difference. Dr. Hari had cut a thin line at my knees. I stared at the line, confused.

The doctors were still looking at my legs. Without saying anything, Dr. Hari grabbed my calf. Another doctor pulled on my thigh. Pain, like fire, shot through my legs. I wanted to throw their hands off me. I wanted to scream into the silence. I wanted to tell them that my legs would not straighten, no matter how hard they pulled. This was a bitter sauce.

The doctors pried my thigh and my calf a little further apart. They placed a wooden rod at the back of my thigh to stop my leg from folding in on itself. Next, they layered plaster back onto my knee, sculpting it into place.

Dr. Hari pushed his glasses up his nose and looked at me seriously. "Whatever you do, don't take this rod out," he warned. I hated that rod. Hated the plaster. Hated this sauce.

The doctors did the same thing with my other leg. When they finished, they lifted me off the table and set me in my wheelchair. Someone pushed me back to my room. I didn't see anything. I didn't see the other girls, or the people nodding at me. I closed my face. There were no smiles left in me.

That night I tried to sleep but my legs burned. I imagined pulling the wooden rods out and tearing the plaster off. I didn't want my legs to be straight. I didn't want any of this. I had only wanted to find a place where I belonged—a place where I would be safe.

For days I didn't talk to anyone, not even Mama. My hope died. Even my tongue died inside my mouth. But eventually, the ache in my legs started to ease. Mama began sitting gently on my bed, telling stories to make me smile. "Remember those games you used to play in Shahalia?" she asked.

I thought about tossing the avocado seed in the air and picking up rocks like a game of jacks. But Mama wasn't talking about that game.

"Don't you remember how many times you snuck away from the house?"

I smiled, remembering my trips to the spring to fetch water. I could still feel the cold splashing down my back.

"You'll be a tall person now!" Mama laughed and started drumming her hand on the edge of the bed to mimic the thumping of crutches. "You'll be walking on crutches! I'll hear you, wherever you go!"

Chapter 34

I learned to count days. Soon, I realized that Thursday came every week, and, every Thursday, Mama pushed me back to kinesiology where the terrible machine buzzed, and the doctors pried my legs a little straighter. For days afterward, I lay in bed with the pain soaring through my legs.

One morning, I was stretched out in bed, staring hopelessly at the chipped beige walls when I heard a sharp knock at the door. The sudden sound startled me. For a minute, I was back in Shahalia lying on a woven mat, with our neighbors hissing warnings through our wobbly wooden door. But then I realized I was safe at the Centre.

There was another insistent knock on the door. "Come out! We need you in the kitchen," a man's voice called from the other side of the door. I looked over at the other beds, but they were empty.

Me? Does he truly want me? What use can I be to anyone? I wondered. I climbed nervously into my wheelchair and pushed myself toward the kitchen. When I reached the door of the kitchen, I heard voices inside. "Hodi," I called cautiously. A man ambled over to the doorway. He was limping on one leg.

"You've come," he said as he nodded approvingly. The man introduced himself as Papa Laloir. In the kitchen, there was a wooden table, a sink with running water, and giant pots hanging from the ceiling above. Papa Laloir called me over to the table and pointed at a basin of dry beans. They looked familiar, like all the beans I'd sorted in Shahalia. I looked at my hands and back at the beans. I knew how to sort beans. After the beans came the potatoes that needed to be peeled and the onions that were waiting to be chopped.

As I worked, I snuck glances around. There was a woman named Da Georgette. She told me that she wasn't a patient at the Centre anymore. She was a worker, and this was her job. She had powdered cheeks and dark eyebrows and bright lipstick, and every time she stood to walk on her crutches, she wrapped her fine kikwembe proudly around her waist. With every step, Da Georgette's leg braces squeaked under her generous size. She was strong and confident, and she ran that kitchen as though it were her own.

"Argentine, you've really helped us today!" Papa Laloir said when the work was done. And even Da Georgette paused to nod at me. For that moment in the kitchen, I was somebody. I had something to offer. And when I returned to the dormitory, I tried to hold my head high like Da Georgette. Maybe I could be a person of meaning.

The next morning, as I lay in bed, I glanced out the window and noticed a shape passing by. It was Papa Laloir on his way to the kitchen. I shoved the curtain aside and rapped my knuckles on the glass of the window, flailing my hands until Papa Laloir came over.

As soon as he neared the window, I widened my eyes and chided, "Kweli, Papa Laloir! Really! Have you forgotten me already?" He chuckled at my exaggerated voice and bowed his head in greeting as he headed off to the kitchen for the day. I stayed there, watching for more friends to pass by. Soon, I saw Da Georgette swaying across the courtyard. I raised my head like her.

I had made an important discovery. Even when I was trapped in my bed, I learned I wasn't alone. My window was like a doorway to the world. I stopped staring at the beige wall in front of me. Instead, I watched through the window, waiting to pounce on anyone that God sent my way.

Chapter 35

They say that hunger is a great teacher, and Mama became hunger's best student. While I was learning to help in the kitchen, Mama was fighting for survival. The Centre provided meals for patients but not for the caregivers. Mama was expected to provide for both herself and Soleil.

A bare patch of ground had been set aside where the caregivers could cook and wash. But even lighting a cooking fire presented a problem for Mama. In Shahalia, Mama had gathered firewood in the pori. Here at the Centre, there were no trees. We were in a city filled with rocks and too many people. At first, it seemed there was nowhere to find wood for a fire, but soon Mama learned that on the other side of the Centre, there was a workshop where men cut wood into crutches. Strewn outside the workshop, Mama found small splinters of wood.

In their hunger, the caregivers shared whatever they had. They lit fires, one from another, just as we had back in Shahalia. Food was flavored with borrowed pinches of salt. Slowly, Mama was learning the economy of the Centre. She learned how to run errands in exchange for tomatoes and how to form alliances that kept the hunger from rising.

When Mama left the Centre to go to the market, she also used that time to visit Ma Mukubwa. My uncle was still traveling on the Fuso to Kashuga to buy sorghum, beans, and potatoes. Mama would beg him to carry news back to the village. "Tell my husband that we are at the Centre, and the doctors are treating his daughter," she would say. When the harvest grew ripe and my uncle left for Kashuga, he'd carry my mother's words with him.

When he arrived in Kashuga, my uncle would look for someone from a village near Shahalia, and he'd send Mama's words forward with them.

That was how news traveled in the hills of Masisi—from one villager to another. It might take months to arrive, but we knew that our message would eventually reach my father and brothers. It was a system respected by villagers everywhere. We carried words to each other like we carried water to those dying of thirst.

Mama and I couldn't stop wondering about my brothers. We waited desperately for news from my uncle. When Mama went to the market, she sometimes went to Birere instead of Virunga. Birere was the crowded neighborhood where buses and trucks arrived from Masisi. Mama would go to the market in Birere so that she could pass by those buses, looking for a familiar face or an accent that carried her back to the hills where she'd grown up as a child. "I'm the daughter of Pastor Bigega in Mariba," she'd explain. If she was lucky, the person might tell her how they had seen one of her sons the other day. Espoir was doing well, we heard. But someone else told us that Ushindi's face was thin. And Tera, who my mother had left back in Shahalia, was suffering the worst of all.

In the long afternoons, my mother sometimes curled on my bed, careful not to jostle my plaster-covered legs. She'd tell me about her trips to the market—about any news she had found there. We'd talk of my brothers. Most of all, she'd look for stories that would make me laugh and forget the pain in my legs.

But I knew that my mother was worried about my brothers. I was worried too. "I'll always return," Mama had promised all of us so many times. My brothers were waiting. My father was waiting.

"You have to forget what you've left behind," Dr. Hari had said when we first arrived. And Mama had agreed.

But no one forgets what they've left behind.

Chapter 36

On Thursdays, the doctors continued straightening my legs. I dreaded going to kinesiology and couldn't eat for days in advance. I could feel my body growing thin, retreating into itself. My sprouting breasts vanished. My monthly blood stopped. When they laid me out on the treatment table, I would ask myself where my body had gone. But finally, I started to see the difference. My legs were starting to straighten. My friend, Bunyere, studied my legs and declared, "Argentine, one day you'll be walking."

Bunyere meant those words as an encouragement, but they twisted my stomach in worried knots.

"What if I can't walk? What if I'm not strong enough?" I asked Bunyere as she sat in her metal kinga. Bunyere's back was crooked like mine, and she had been at the Centre longer than any of the other girls. Years ago, the doctors had straightened her legs and fit her with a plastic corset, hoping to keep her back straight. But she had never learned to walk, and the doctors had given her a kinga instead. By the time I arrived at the Centre, Bunyere had been happily driving her kinga.

I remembered what the doctors had said about me when I first arrived. "She'll be like Bunyere," they had said. At the time I didn't know what that meant—whether it was a compliment or a curse. And when I met Bunyere later that week, it had seemed like a compliment. Bunyere seemed well to me. There was no bitterness in her body. Her face wasn't long with sorrow. She had so many friends, and she could wheel herself wherever she wanted inside the Centre. To me, she was free.

But every time Dr. Hari straightened my legs, he told me that I'd be walking soon, and I didn't want to disappoint him. I could see the way the doctors shook their heads at Bunyere, as though she hadn't tried hard enough. This terrified me. I didn't want Dr. Hari to shake his head at me. I had to learn to walk. I was a person in need of help, and I couldn't afford to disappoint anyone.

"It's time to stand you up," a nun named Mother Thérèse told me one day when I arrived at kinesiology. She pointed me out the door and onto the patio to a set of parallel bars. My heart left my stomach, and I spun around in my wheelchair, looking for Mama. She was trailing behind us. Everyone looked happy, but my heart was filled with dread. My legs were still covered in plaster, and my back was still crooked like Bunyere's.

"Courage," Mother Thérèse said, hoisting me by my armpits. She propped me onto the parallel bars. My fingers clutched at the smooth wood. I was carrying all my weight on my shoulders and wrists. My plaster-covered legs dangled somewhere beneath me. I wasn't standing, but I was upright in a way that I had never been before.

"Look at Argentine!" one of my friends hooted, followed by shouts and whistles. Everyone in the room clapped like mothers watching a baby stand.

"You've really straightened out! You'll be getting married any day now," someone joked. I was trying desperately to hold my back still, but it was already wobbling as though there was nothing but air inside me.

Everyone else seemed thrilled with my progress. Mama was clapping and thanking God. "Bring a camera! I'll pay for a photo!" she cried. As we waited for someone to fetch a camera, I looked at my plaster legs, sticking out from the shorts I was wearing. I couldn't take a picture in shorts. "Quick Mama! Bring a kitenge for me!"

Mama grabbed a yellow kitenge that she used for carrying Soleil. She wrapped it around my waist, and I felt the worn fabric drape my body. It was what I had prayed for back in Shahalia. Every time my father brought clothes for our family, he brought black shorts for me. "You will get dirty anyway," he'd say, and he was right. But what child wants to wear black? I had never stopped dreaming of being tall enough to wear a colorful kitenge wrapped at my waist, and now here I was, at last.

"You're a tall person now!" Mama called out happily, and someone clicked a picture.

Chapter 37

It was only a few days later when Mama whispered a secret to me. "Argentine, it's time for me to go," she said into the darkness. "I have to check on your brothers."

The air fell out of the room. I couldn't breathe. We had been at the Centre for nearly a year, and I couldn't imagine my life at the Centre without Mama. She was the one who knew how to do everything. She knew how to talk to the men in the offices and how to send messages back to Shahalia. I wanted to cling to Mama and beg her to stay. But I thought about Tera and Espoir and Ushindi. My little brothers. They were waiting for Mama. It was my turn to let her go.

Leaving the Centre wouldn't be easy for Mama. She couldn't just walk out the gate and leave me behind. I couldn't stay at the Centre without a caregiver. Mama turned to the other women—the ones who shared pinches of salt and sparks of fire. They had become like the roots that grow beneath trees, weaving in and out of each other's lives.

One of the women, Mama Solange, offered to take care of me. But even with someone else to care for me, my mother still needed permission to leave the Centre.

That was the life of a caregiver. They lived caught in between. Their legs were not plastered, and they were free to walk out the gate. They could go to the market or visit friends nearby. But they needed permission to travel home.

"Have mercy on me. My other children are sick. I'll come back soon," Mama said to the men in the offices, and they gave her permission to go, but one of the men added a warning. "If you don't come back soon, we will throw Argentine into the street."

When Mama recounted that warning to me, I thought about the rocky streets of Goma. I had been lost in those streets before, but at least I had been able to crawl. Now, with the plaster on my legs, I couldn't even crawl. If they threw me into the street now, I'd die there.

The next morning, my mother started preparing to leave, but before she could pack her bags, the situation changed. Mama Solange arrived in my dormitory room explaining that she wouldn't be able to take care of me. She and her daughter were being sent home. The doctors had said there was nothing more they could do for her daughter.

Mama nodded her head in understanding, and soon she found another caregiver willing to stay with me. But now there was a different dilemma. Mama Solange was asking for my mother's help. "Before you leave on your journey, won't you accompany me and my daughter back to Rwanda?" Mama Solange asked. She explained how they lived over the border on a hill called Rubavu. "I can't carry my daughter home by myself," Mama Solange pleaded.

My mother stood there. She must have been thinking about my father and brothers back in Masisi. They were waiting. But standing in the doorway was Mama Solange. My mother couldn't say no. She put down her bundle. "I will help you first," she agreed.

The next day, I took Soleil from my mother's arms and watched Mama leave for Rwanda. "I'll return before evening," Mama promised. They left, with my mother carrying Mama Solange's younger child on her back and Mama Solange carrying her nine-year old daughter—the one the doctors could no longer help.

All day I sat at the Centre thinking about Mama. I couldn't even survive one day without her. When the sun started to set, I wondered where Mama was. They'd be closing the gates for the evening soon. Mama walked into the dining room just as we finished our dinner. I expected her hands to be empty, but she was carrying a bundle. When she caught me staring at the bundle, Mama widened her eyes to hush me. "Tonight, I'll tell you," she whispered.

That evening, while I was lying in bed, Mama told me how she and Mama Solange had walked across the border and taken bicycle taxis up a hill. Skinny boys had peddled those bicycles as far as they could, until the path grew so steep that they could peddle no further.

Then the two women had climbed off the bicycles and started to hike. Finally, they reached a small hut on the top of the mountain. In the hut, Mama sank into a chair to rest, and Mama Solange ducked behind a curtain. There was thumping and movement, and Mama Solange emerged with a pair of children's shoes. "Take these with you. Maybe they will fit one of your boys back in Shahalia," Mama Solange said. She left again and came back with a warm sweatshirt. And then another pair of shoes. And then some more clothing, until my mother had a whole sack of clothes and shoes to take to Shahalia.

Back at the Centre, my mother finished her story and pointed at the sack she had set at our feet. "You see?" she said proudly. "I have something to bring home now. I won't be returning to Shahalia empty-handed."

That night, I began to wonder what would happen to Mama when she returned to Shahalia. My father had never wanted us to leave, and now Mama was returning after a year. What would he say?

The next morning, Mama announced that she still wasn't ready to leave for Shahalia. She was going to visit Pastor Amani and his wife first. That evening, she came back with more clothes and a container of homemade lotion from Mama Pastor.

The following day, Mama said she was ready to leave. She opened her sack and pulled out a new shirt for Soleil and a new pair of shoes for herself. She smoothed her hair back and rubbed the homemade oil into her skin. Someone had given her a new purse, and she tucked photos of me inside.

I had no idea what my mother might face in Shahalia. We'd left with nothing, and now she was returning with something. I hoped it would be enough to appease my father.

As my mother walked out the door, Mama Internat clucked disapprovingly, as though she had seen this situation a thousand times. "She's going to abandon you here," Mama Internat muttered.

I knew Mama Internat was wrong. Mama would never abandon me. She would come back. She always came back.

Chapter 38

Weeks passed, and my mother did not return. Mama Internat circled around me like a hawk. "Did you mop this floor yet? Why isn't your room clean?" she asked as she thundered through our dormitory.

I couldn't stop thinking about Mama. I ate ugali and sauce that stuck in my throat. Every time that I swallowed, I wondered if Mama had something to eat. I prayed that my father had welcomed Mama back, but I wasn't sure if that was possible. How does a man explain the absence of a wife who has been gone for a year—especially one who left three of her sons behind?

I tried to keep my room as clean as I could. In the mornings, I mopped the floor with a rag, my body doubled over as I sat in my wheelchair. I prayed that Mama would return. I breathed prayers in and out like air. I went to the chapel and sang songs that were prayers. At night, even my dreams were prayers for my mother.

As the weeks passed, Mama Internat's questions grew sharper. "Argentine, where is your mother? Why hasn't she come back?"

"I don't know," I answered softly. It was the truth. I didn't know where my mother was. I didn't know if she was back in Shahalia or if she had been attacked along the way. Maybe she was at my grandfather's farm fetching Espoir, or maybe she was in Nyanzale looking for Ushindi. I had no idea where she was.

Mama Internat narrowed her eyes at me. "What family do you have in Goma?"

"We have no family in Goma," I said, repeating the words as though they were true. Mama and I had said those words so many times that they felt like the truth. I knew that Ma Mukubwa and her husband were in Goma, but they had never visited me at the Centre.

I could have told Mama Internat about my aunt and uncle in Goma. But what good would that have done? The staff at the Centre would have demanded my aunt and uncle come to visit me—that they contribute to my expenses or take me home. But I learned long ago that you can only ask of people what they are ready to give.

"What family do you have in Goma?" Mama Internat demanded again.

"There is no one," I said, and when I went to sleep that night, I knew it was true. I was alone in this place. I thought about the girls I had seen on my first day, with their hair in braids and beads—they were from Goma. I was from Masisi. My hair was braided into simple rows. I had no extensions or beads. I had no visitors to bring me those things.

I was not like the girls from Goma. If Mama Internat kicked me out of the Centre, I would have nowhere to go. I'd be lost in the streets of Goma again. I could already feel the slick black mud on my hands and the sharp smell of petrol biting my nose.

Every day, Mama Internat squinted her eyes at me. "Where's your mother? Does she think she can abandon you here?" she clucked louder and louder. I knew Mama would never abandon me, but I wondered if something had happened to her. How would I know if she'd been attacked on the road to Mweso just like her sister?

Finally, one day, as I was cleaning the floor, Mama and Soleil arrived. I threw myself into Mama's arms. I was so happy to see Mama and Soleil that it took some time to notice the girl standing next to Mama. It was Magambo, our pastor's daughter from Shahalia, the quiet one. I flashed a big smile at Magambo, trying to make her feel comfortable, but she continued looking nervously at all the bright lights.

That night, Mama told me about her journey to Shahalia. She told me how she had left the Centre carrying Soleil on her back and the bundle of gifts on her head. She retraced our path, riding on the back of a truck and sleeping at Majinaa's house in Mweso. Just as she was preparing to leave Mweso, she had seen some friends from Shahalia.

"Mama Argentine! Could that be you?" one of the women called out.

"Ehh! You are looking good! Your face is shining!" they said, marveling at my mother's skin, rubbed soft with Mama Pastor's oil.

"And what about your daughter? How is Argentine?"

My mother opened her new purse and showed them the photo of me in that yellow kitenge standing at the parallel bars.

"Mungu we! Look at Argentine! She's standing!" the women exclaimed. They linked arms with my mother and offered to walk back to Shahalia together.

As they climbed the hill called Bushanga, my mother noticed a worried expression on some of the women's faces. The group grew quiet until one of the women confessed, "We don't know if your husband will take you back. People have been telling him that you left because he was too poor. They said that you went to lie on other men's mattresses."

My mother listened silently, clutching her purse with the photos—proof of where she had been. The women walked on in silence. When they reached our house, with the avocado tree, the women hugged my mother goodbye and wished her success. "We'll pray for you," they promised.

Inside our house, Mama found Tera at home. He'd grown tall and thin, like a child who has no mother—but he was alive. Mama heated water for him and rubbed the homemade lotion into his skin. My father wasn't home, so she started to cook. Late in the night, my father ducked inside. He jumped back in surprise. "You've come home now?" he cried out. He started checking the corners of the room. "And where is that child of yours? Where have you left Argentine?"

My mother smiled calmly back at him, keeping her long forehead smooth. "God has blessed us," she answered, and then she began to explain about my treatment at the Centre.

"But the money," my father interrupted. "The money for this treatment...where will we get it?"

"We don't need any money. God has provided..." Mama insisted.

My father shook his head, still spinning around, unable to understand, "But you left with nothing," he sputtered.

My mother opened her purse and took out her photos. She showed him the picture of me standing at the parallel bars with the yellow kitenge wrapped at my waist.

My father looked at the photo and jumped. "Is that Argentine? Standing? Is that really our child?" He whistled and touched the photo again. My father stood there for a long time, looking at the photo and clicking his tongue. "Can it be true?"

Mama showed him another photo with me sitting in a wheelchair. "God be praised," he said, and he looked at my mother, as though he was seeing her for the first time. He must have been remembering all those days of fasting, and all those nights he found my mother on her knees in prayer. Finally, he spoke in amazement. "This was you. God answered your prayers," he said to my mother.

The following day, my mother went to Nyanzale to look for Ushindi. Then she hiked to my grandfather's farm to fetch Espoir. Days later, she returned with all her boys. Their faces were hollow, and their skin had turned to ash, but they were safe. After each boy had bathed, Mama took out the container of homemade oil and rubbed it into their skin. Even my father rubbed his skin soft with that oil.

Next, my mother opened her sack and pulled out shoes and clothes for her husband and sons. After that, the bundle was still full. On Sunday, she carried it over to the church, and out of it she pulled a piece of clothing for each family in our congregation. Every family went home with something that day. In my mother's sack, there was enough for everyone.

Back at the Centre, my mother told me all the news from Shahalia. I tried to ask Magambo for news as well. "How is Bébé? How is the choir?" The longer I talked to Magambo, the more I began to wonder why she was there. After a while, Mama confessed. Magambo was there to be my caregiver. Mama was planning to leave again.

Chapter 39

When Mama left the Centre the second time, I tried to focus on other things. I was happy to have Magambo with me, even though she was still quiet. The name *Magambo* comes from *amagambo* which means *words* in Kinyarwanda, and I would tease my quiet friend about her ill-fitting name.

"Why did they give you that name? They should have given it to me!" I would joke, and Magambo would smile without saying anything.

Of course, I had only recently learned where my own name came from. One day, I was visiting an electrician who worked at the Centre. He had a television, and I'd never seen one of those boxes before. On it, a soccer game was playing.

The electrician pointed to the box and said, "Argentine, there's your team!"

Confused, I squinted at the box filled with fuzzy motion. I saw no one who resembled me. Finally, the electrician explained that a team named Argentina was playing. That's how I learned that my father had named me after a soccer team. Magambo wasn't the only one with an ill-fitting name.

At the Centre, there was always so much to learn. In one building there was a school where the teachers taught reading and writing. When I first started at the school, one of the teachers pointed me into a classroom. I rolled into the room, but I felt like something was missing. Shayo wasn't in my class. Nor was Bunyere. None of my friends were there. When I looked at the students sitting at the other desks, I saw that it was a class of little children and me. All my memories from Shahalia came flooding back. I'd already failed at school once. I was too old to fail again.

When I first arrived at the Centre, Sister Louise had asked me if I had ever gone to school before. "No," I had told her, "I've never gone to school before." It had felt like the truth. I barely remembered anything from the school in Shahalia. It was a period of my life that I had tried to forget.

But now, I was sitting in this classroom next to six-year-old children. The teacher asked if I could write the alphabet. And the answer was *yes*. Maybe I had learned something in Shahalia.

The teacher transferred me to a different classroom. Shayo and Bunyere smiled at me when I entered the new room. This was where I belonged. I joined my friends enthusiastically, but soon I realized that I was far behind. The teacher's words came sharp like a machete.

"Where did you grow up? Can't you learn anything?" she chided.

I was so desperate to make my teachers happy that sometimes I resorted to a little extra help. As soon as the teacher turned her back to write on the chalkboard, I would whisper to my friends, "Does anyone know the answer?" But I always whispered too loudly. The teacher would twist back to me, the words still caught in my mouth.

At the end of the school year, there was a proclamation ceremony, and the director announced the names of every student in order—the first student, the second student, the third student, and so on. I wasn't the first student, or the second, or the third—but I didn't mind. The numbers weren't so important to me. I was more interested in the handwritten note on the bottom of the report card. That's where the teachers commented on our ability to vivre en société, to live in society. This seemed like the most important assessment to me. They would write 'B' for bien—good, or 'TB' for très bien—very good. There must have been other letters also, but I remember the 'B' because that's what I got. And I remember the 'TB' because that is what Shayo got.

That first year, Shayo tried to hide her success from me. After the ceremony, we raced in our wheelchairs back toward the dormitory. As we moved, I hid my report card under my leg where no one could see it. Then, I begged Shayo to show me her report card, which was still flapping in her hands, impossible to deny.

Shayo smirked back at me. "Let me see yours first," she countered, but I shrugged and lifted my hands to show they were empty. Shayo turned away in her wheelchair, but I could still see the report card in her hand. "What did you get?" I pestered until she stretched the report card out so that I could read it. There it was, written on the bottom: *TB*. Très bien.

I pulled out my own report card and showed it to her. There was a lonely 'B' on the bottom. I was *good*, but not *very good*. "Wait until next year," I promised. "Next year, I'll live in society better than everyone else!"

Chapter 40

My caregiver, Magambo, didn't stay at the Centre very long. Her family requested that she return home, and Mama came back to the Centre again. When Mama arrived, she was still carrying Soleil on her back. She slid him to the ground and showed me how he could walk. As I congratulated Soleil, I noticed another boy standing next to Mama.

"Ushindi, is that you?" I asked, reaching my arms toward my five-year-old brother. His eyes were big as he looked at me in my wheelchair with my plaster legs stretched straight in front of me. The last time he'd seen me; I'd been crawling on the dirt path in Shahalia.

Mama told me that Ushindi had been sick, and she couldn't bear to leave him, so she'd brought both Ushindi and Soleil with her. Soon, Mama Internat raced over. "Really, Mama Argentine! Do you think this is your own personal living arrangement? This is no place for two children!" Mama Internat boomed.

Mama fell to her knees and bowed her head. "Have mercy on me." Mama Internat's face didn't soften, so Mama continued. "I'll find somewhere else for this one to sleep," she said pointing at Ushindi.

That's how my mother became like a cat again—carrying her children in her teeth and hiding them under bushes. Mama asked a friend who lived nearby to let Ushindi sleep at her house at night. The woman agreed, as long as during the day, Ushindi returned to the Centre so Mama could feed him.

As the days passed, Mama scrambled to feed herself and both of my brothers. Sometimes, she left Soleil and Ushindi with me and carried big sacks of sweet potatoes on her head over the border to Rwanda. She brought fresh squash back to appease Mama Internat.

I asked my mother how she learned to do all of this, crossing the border and changing money. She said Mama Solange had shown her how to do all of this, on that bicycle trip to the top of the mountain. My mother's small kindness to Mama Solange had repaid itself over and over.

Still, despite my mother's efforts, we lived waiting for Mama Internat to erupt and send us all home. We lived at the mercy of others, just as we always had. My mother swept and mopped in the mornings, all the time trying to think of ways to keep Mama Internat happy.

Around that time, Mama Internat began walking through the dormitory, lost in another problem, shaking her head and saying, "Now what will I do?"

My mother waited patiently. She mopped the floors and prayed aloud that God would send Mama Internat in her direction. Eventually, Mama Internat wandered toward my mother.

"Have you heard the news?" Mama Internat whispered, leaning in and lowering her voice as though she were trusting my mother with an important secret. "We have a new patient arriving with no caregiver. I don't know who is going to take care of this new patient." Mama Internat let her voice trail off.

Mama looked up. "I will take care of the new patient," she offered.

"Really? Will you do that for me?" Mama Internat exclaimed, her face relaxing into a broad smile.

That's when my mother saw her moment. She shifted her body a little and moved her head toward my brothers. "But, you see, I do have these two young boys here..."

"Oh, your sons? They are no trouble at all," Mama Internat replied, her smile wide. "They can both stay at the Centre! I'll even cook them some squash!"

Chapter 41

I was impressed by my mother's cleverness. She was both fast and patient—like a cat, lying in wait.

I wasn't fast or patient. With my legs covered in plaster, I was more like a baby goat, awkward and prone to falling. Ever since I started using the parallel bars, I knew that I had a problem. My hips were sticking out too far, and the doctors sent me to physical therapy.

In the physical therapy room, there were rows of tables. I lay on my stomach while the doctors and nurses tied straps around my hips trying to flatten me out. Dr. Lungel worked in the physical therapy room, and he cinched those straps so tight that I wanted to cry. Mother Thérèse and Mama Vero also worked in the physical therapy room. Soon, I realized that Mama Vero was in her fifties. She never tied anything too tight. "Mama Vero, will you help me today?" I would call eagerly as soon as I rolled through the door. I was determined to charm my way to survival in that physical therapy room.

There was one good thing about physical therapy. I was never alone. Shayo, my twin, would be on the table next to me and beside her would be an older boy named Blaise. After some time on the table, my hips would ache from the unfamiliar position, and I'd beg to be released from the exercise. "Mother Thérèse, I need your help!" I would call out, trying to make my voice sweet. She'd come over, wearing her blue habit and long robe, with her wooden crucifix dangling in front of me.

"Why Argentine, what could possibly be wrong?" she'd ask.

"I can't take it anymore."

"Oh no, Argentine, you can't possibly be tired already! Look at your friends! Look at Blaise and Shayo! They aren't tired at all," she'd say, and off she would go.

But that wouldn't stop me. As soon as Mother Thérèse had moved on to another task, I would try my luck with gentle Mama Vero. "Mama Vero! Mama Vero! I can't be patient anymore!"

Mama Vero would look at me indulgently, as though she hadn't heard me talking to Mother Thérèse. "Argentine, you can't be tired already," she would answer. "Look at Blaise over there. He never gets tired." And then Mama Vero would move on.

I'd squint my eyes at Blaise. He was big and strong, and he'd been doing these exercises for months.

"Shayo," I'd whisper, "tell Blaise to help us out. Tell him to start crying. If he cries like me, they'll let us rest."

But it was no use. Blaise would grin back at me, and never once did he cry.

Months later, after Blaise had already finished his physical therapy, I saw him again. We were both gathered outside watching a volleyball game. Youth from the neighborhood had started a volleyball team, and they practiced on the grass at the Centre. Before the games, some of the players would race through the dormitory, inviting patients to watch the match.

I loved those volleyball games. My friends and I would gather by the spectator bench ready to cheer on our favorite players. As soon as the game began, we stopped thinking about kinesiology. We forgot about physical therapy. We were no longer a group of patients with disabilities; we were a roaring crowd of fans.

As I was sitting there watching the volleyball match, I heard Blaise's voice over the crowd. "Ehh, Argentine, is that you?" he joked as though he couldn't quite remember. A grin spread across his face. "Do you still complain so much?" he asked, his eyes laughing.

"Me?" I responded, pressing my hand to my heart and widening my eyes in exaggeration. I turned to my friends gathered around. "Do you all know Blaise? He's so hard-hearted. All he had to do was cry a little, and he could have saved us all!" I announced.

Blaise laughed. So did I. It's how we learned to survive at the Centre, laughing together at the pain we all shared.

Chapter 42

My mother couldn't stay at the Centre forever. I was only gradually realizing this. Tera, Espoir, and my father were still back in Shahalia, and Mama could never bring all of them to the Centre. I began to realize that Mama had never intended to follow Dr. Hari's instructions—to forget what she left behind. She had only been biding her time, waiting to spring into action when the right opportunity arose.

At last, she found what she'd been waiting for—someone to care for me. I don't know how Mama arranged it, but Ma Muloko arrived at the Centre. She was my 'little mother', one of my mother's half-sisters from Nyanzale. Ma Muloko was only four years older than me, and she had always been kind. She and her sisters used to visit our house in Shahalia. As young girls they carried me on their backs all the way to Nyanzale.

Mama left me at the Centre with Ma Muloko. "I have to return to Shahalia," she said. This time, I wasn't so worried when she left. I was feeling strong and confident. I had so many friends at the Centre now. And I was starting to believe that one day they'd take the plaster off my legs, and I'd be a tall person. I could almost hear my crutches thudding down the hallway. Shayo was already walking on crutches, and I thought I could become like her.

But one day, as we were lying on the physical therapy tables, Shayo scrunched her face at my protruding hips. "They'll operate on your hips soon," Shayo predicted.

My blood ran cold. An operation. This was not what I was prepared for. At the Centre, the doctors sometimes sent patients across Goma to the hospital for operations. I had gone to visit other girls in that terrifying place. My friend, Denise, had a leg shattered by bullets, and when I went to visit her at the hospital, I found her sweating in bed with her leg strapped in the air.

"Will you ever come back to the Centre?" I had asked Denise in a shaky voice, and she had promised she would. A few months later, Denise had returned to the Centre, and now she was walking on crutches. But there had been other patients who had been taken to the hospital, and sometimes they never returned.

I begged Ma Muloko to send news to Masisi and tell Mama to return to the Centre. But I knew the message would travel slowly, and I'd be going to the hospital long before Mama returned.

It was only a few weeks later that Ma Muloko and I left for the hospital in one of the Centre's transportation vans. There were no seats in the back of the van, only a metal floor with space for a cot. I heard the gate of the Centre closing behind us and prayed that I'd be one of the people who returned one day. When we arrived at the hospital, it was dark. We slept on narrow beds and waited for them to take me to the operating room in the morning.

After the surgery, I awoke to the sound of voices saying my name. "She'll be okay," I heard the doctors telling Ma Muloko. Warm milky tea trickled down my throat. I slept.

Suddenly, the world jolted. The ceiling began to move. There were flashes of blue sky and sunlight, and the sound of car doors opening. I was still foggy from anesthesia, and no words came to my mouth. I tasted only the milky tea on my tongue. But I wanted to say something. *Let me stay here!* I wanted to cry. The movement was sending jolts of pain up my body. I wanted to beg Ma Muloko to stop them from moving me. But Ma Muloko was a village girl like me. What could she say to the doctors?

The engine rumbled, and we started to move. I couldn't see the city, but I could feel it. In my back. In my hips. In my legs. I felt every rock in the road, every pothole, and every tear rolling down my face, until I heard the big metal gate creak open, and we returned to the Centre.

Chapter 43

Water splashed down my back. I was at the spring in Sha-halia with Gasirimu pouring cold water over my shoulders. Then I was at Sister Louise's compound with water that flowed from a tap. In every dream I was covered with water, but I awoke to find myself lying flat on my back in the Salle des Malades—the room for sick people.

In the Salle des Malades, I was trapped under plaster from my chest to my toes, with only a space open at my backside for a chamber pot. I couldn't sit up. I could only lie on my back and stare at the ceiling. Sweat trickled under my plaster. I wanted to tear that plaster off, but doubts turned in my head. What would happen when they removed the plaster? What bitter sauce was waiting for me next?

After a month, the doctors removed the plaster from my upper body. Weeks later, they called me back to kinesiology. "Are you ready to stand?" they asked. Without waiting for an answer, the terrible machine began to whir, and my stomach lurched. Fingers pressed into my shoulders. Dr. Hari cut the plaster on my leg in half, opening the pieces like a shell to reveal my skinny leg. It was dirty, with the skin peeling off. This was not the leg that I had imagined. It looked worse than it had before.

Horrified by the sight of my leg, I asked Dr. Hari what I could do. "If I rub oil on the skin, will it grow smooth again?" I asked, thinking of Mama Pastor's homemade lotion. No one answered. The doctors were focused on other tasks. They had removed the plaster from both legs, and now they were trying to fit braces onto my skinny limbs.

Before my surgery they had measured my legs, and now there was a pair of metal braces for me. The braces had thick blocks of wood that buckled onto my feet like shoes, and metal posts that rose to the crease in my thighs. The doctors buckled the leather straps around my legs. Sharp, cold metal bit into my skin. Someone lifted me and propped me on the parallel bars. I stood. My hips were somewhere beneath me. I wondered if they were straight now. Everyone clapped and whistled, as they had the first time I stood there.

"You're looking good! You'll be married any day," someone shouted again. Papa Ruzi, one of the men who worked at the Centre, walked by and called out, "Argentine, you're growing up! We'll be eating beef soon! You can tell those suitors to bring the cows straight to my house!"

Usually, I liked to joke, but on this day, I couldn't join the laughter. I was too busy trying to think of a way out of the metal braces. I wanted to go back to the plaster. If only I knew where they had thrown the pieces of my casts, I would send Ma Muloko out in the night to pick up the broken halves so I could tie them back onto my legs.

My God, how I hated those metal braces. But the doctors told me I had to wear them. "You must practice standing. No more sitting in that wheelchair," the doctors would chide every time they saw me. "You won't learn to walk like that!"

My friends and I became very good at escaping the doctors. Mornings at the Centre started with a bell ringing at 7:30. As the doctors arrived for the day, we watched carefully from our wheelchairs, just out of sight.

"Dr. Hari has arrived. Dr. Lungel has arrived," we whispered as we narrated the arrival of every doctor. We were like prey watching the hunters arrive, ready to scatter as soon as they turned their attention to us. None of us wanted to get caught sitting in our wheelchairs, but we also didn't want the pain of standing, so instead we raced out of sight. In our wheelchairs, we spun through the corridor, past the kitchen and back toward the classrooms. The shortcut past the kitchen was steep, and we had to push our wheels as hard as we could, but it was worth the effort to avoid the doctors.

When I could escape the doctors no longer, I did my best to please them. I would put on my leg braces and convince Ma Muloko to join me in the long corridor. When no one was looking, she'd lift me out of my wheelchair and prop me against the wall, and I'd practice standing there with my palms pressed against the chipped cement and my wheelchair empty beside me.

Just before the doctors arrived, Ma Muloko would slyly disappear, leaving me standing there on my own. "Argentine, you're standing all by yourself!" the doctors would say as they passed by, even though they must have seen my back shaking and my hands grabbing the wall. They must have known that I couldn't stand by myself, and that Ma Muloko was hovering somewhere nearby. But they never mentioned any of that. In-stead, they congratulated me enthusiastically, and their words kept me standing there a little bit longer.

One of the workers at the Centre was a man named Papa Katenge. He had a soft voice, and he never gave up on anyone. "Binti zangu—my daughters" he'd sigh when he caught us sit-ting in our wheelchairs. His words were so gentle that I al-ways tried my best for Papa Katenge, but I still couldn't stand on my crutches. Crutches were nothing like parallel bars. They were only pieces of wood flung to the side. They had no power. They offered no strength. Crutches depended entirely on the strength of the person who wielded them.

And I wasn't strong.

When I tried to stand on my crutches, my back wobbled like porridge, and I collapsed onto the hard, cement floor. At night, I thought of how I'd first arrived at the Centre. "This child will never walk," the woman doctor had said in French, pointing at my back. She had been right. I'd never learn to walk on crutches. My back was too weak, and the metal braces made my legs too heavy to move.

My head spun with thoughts. When you have a disability, you think a lot. Your body refuses to move, so your brain runs faster trying to catch up. But, this time, there was nowhere for my brain to run. There were no other solutions. The doctors left no other options. I had to learn to walk on my crutches.

I returned to kinesiology, determined to take a step on my own. Mama Vero hoisted me up, and I balanced precariously on my crutches. I could feel Mama Vero's hand on my back. It gave me the courage to place my crutches in front of me and throw my heavy legs forward.

"Argentine, you're doing it!" Mama Vero cried and started to pull her hand away.

"Don't leave me!" I wailed.

"You're walking all by yourself," she promised, but that was not what I wanted to hear. I didn't want to walk alone. I'd never wanted that.

"No! No! Walk with me!" I begged, and Mama Vero returned one hand to my back. I heaved my crutches forward and threw my legs again. Mama Vero walked beside me—tugging at my shirt to let me know she was still there.

Chapter 44

We never know the day when disaster will arrive. January 17 started off as a good day. It was a holiday. None of the workers were coming to the Centre that day, and I was happy that no one would be telling me to practice walking. I slept late in the morning, and when I awoke, I stared out the window, confused. Something was wrong. There was no sun in the sky. In Africa, you know it is morning by the sun, but, on this day, the sky was blank and empty and grey as a pot.

I buckled my braces onto my legs and greeted Shayo, who had also slept late. We climbed in our wheelchairs and tucked our blankets neatly under the edges of our beds as Mama Internat had taught us. Then we rolled toward the dining room. In the dining room, we found Bunyere, sitting in her metal kinga next to Joli and Habimana.

Joli and Habimana were from Rwanda, and through them I had begun to understand what had happened in Rwanda in 1994. Their parents had been killed. Joli was a girl, younger than me. Both her legs had been amputated, and her brother, Habimana, had brought her across the border to the Centre for treatment. Habimana was already a full-grown man with broad shoulders and a strong, slow voice. Sometimes he would sit in the dining room teaching Bunyere to pronounce words in Kinyarwanda. I thought Bunyere might marry Habimana the way they always huddled together.

When I rolled into the dining room, I found Habimana and Bunyere whispering together. I heard Habimana say something about a volcan, but I didn't understand the French word. I turned to Shayo. "What's a volcan?"

Shayo looked confused as well. The day was quiet. What could be wrong? There was no high-pitched warning cry. No one was banging a spoon on a pot or whispering through doors. Bullets weren't crying. Besides, we were safe at the Centre—safe behind walls and gates.

I shrugged. "Let's check outside," I suggested.

We pushed our wheelchairs out to the veranda and threw our eyes around the compound. Nothing. Everything was blank.

"I'll check over there," I said to Shayo, wheeling myself toward the bench by the volleyball net, where I'd joked with Blaise. No one was at the bench. I heard women's voices coming from the kitchen area, so I pushed myself in that direction. In front of the kitchen, I found several women.

"What's a volcan?" I asked the women.

Their heads jerked up. "How can you not know what a volcan is?" one of the women sputtered. I was starting to become nervous. The woman pointed over the tall, rock wall, "Can't you see? Fire is spilling out of the mountain over there," she said.

My eyes followed the woman's hand, but I saw only a rock wall and the heavy, grey sky. I remembered the flat-topped mountain that rose nearby. But it was only a mountain. How could fire spill from a mountain?

In Shahalia, fire was warmth and safety. When I arrived home after a rainstorm, my mother heated water on a fire to warm my body. In the evenings, we sat by the cooking fire, roasting potatoes and corn and cutting stories. And when my brothers collected firewood in the pori, we prayed only that the fire would light.

"What are you saying?" I asked, even more confused.

The woman stared back at me and shook her head. "Don't you see the grey stuff falling from the sky?"

I looked up, but all I could see was the tin overhang from the roof. I turned away from the women and pushed my wheelchair out into the open air. I looked again. Blank. I turned my palms to the sky. Suddenly, the skin of my palms were covered with grey grit. Fine like salt. Dark like rock. It was everywhere. Materializing on my hands out of nowhere. I'd never seen anything like it before.

"It's true!" I said, brushing my hands together and rolling myself back toward the women. But no one was there to hear me. I had been gone less than five minutes, but now the kitchen was empty, and I was alone.

I have to tell Shayo, I thought, so I pushed myself back toward the dining room. As I crossed the empty corridor, I saw Papa Laloir lilting across the courtyard. He was carrying his son on his back, and he was headed toward the front gate, but I still didn't think anything about it. He could have been going anywhere.

When I returned to the dining room, only Shayo was sitting in her wheelchair in the middle of the big room. The wooden table and benches were empty. Bunyere, Habimana, and Joli had vanished.

"Where's Bunyere? Where's Habimana?" I asked.

"Everyone's gone," Shayo said, throwing her hands toward the empty room. "We're here by ourselves."

"No. It's not possible! We can't be alone!" I said, almost laughing. The Centre was big, and there were always so many people. "I'll go find the others," I promised, and I wheeled out of the dining room again.

I pushed my wheelchair over to the other side of the building. I was thinking of the two men with paralyzed legs who lived down the hall, Papa Jules and Papa Donatien. They couldn't have gone anywhere.

As I steered my wheelchair into their room, I started to relax. Papa Jules was lying in bed. He turned toward me in surprise. "Sister Argentine! Are you still here?" he cried. "Don't you know? Everyone has already left!"

My legs started to tremble.

"But what about Papa Donatien?" I asked, checking the other bed and finding it empty.

"He's gone," Papa Jules said, hurriedly explaining that Papa Donatien's wife had come into their room and hoisted her husband on her back.

I shook my head in disbelief. Papa Donatien's wife was a small woman. How could she carry her husband on her back?

"What about their baby?" I asked.

"She carried the baby on her front, and her husband on her back," Papa Jules insisted.

Nothing made sense on this day. I tried to picture this small woman carrying her husband and baby together. At first it seemed impossible. But then I remembered Mama carrying me up the hill called Gapfura and dragging my brothers beside us.

Suddenly, I felt very alone. Why had I left Shayo? Where was Ma Muloko? Every time I turned my head, more people disappeared. I thanked Papa Jules and pushed my way back to the dining room. I was desperate to find my friends. The air tasted bitter, and it clung to the back of my throat.

When I returned to the dining room, I was relieved to find people there. Shayo was sitting with her younger sister,

Consolata, and my caregiver, Ma Muloko. We were four village girls alone.

We sat in the big, empty dining room and looked at each other silently. A man hurried past the doorway and shouted, "Girls, don't you understand? The volcano is erupting. Look outside the gate! Everyone is running!"

Running? Where are people running to? How do you run from a mountain? I wondered.

We pushed ourselves toward the gate. Grit coated our skin and our clothes. The air was thick with smoke, and it was hard to breathe. The sky above us glowed blood red. The world was ending.

When we arrived at the front gate, we stopped and stared outside. I was shocked. The roads of Goma were always busy, but now they were overflowing with people running in every direction—pushing into each other, dragging their children, carrying mattresses and metal cooking pots on their heads. Deep in my stomach, I was afraid. I had seen people run like this before. I knew that it meant something terrible was coming.

Shayo and I sat at the gate, peering into the street. Usually, I felt confident in my wheelchair. I was an expert. I could move quickly on the cement walkways inside the Centre. But I never left the Centre. There was no place for a wheelchair on the bumpy streets of Goma. Now, as we stared into the panicked crowd, I realized that Shayo and I were stuck. If we pushed ourselves onto the rock-strewn road, our chairs would topple, and we'd be crushed by the crowds. We didn't have our crutches with us and even if we did, we could barely walk. We were trapped, and this time my mother was not coming to save me.

Next to me, Shayo was quietly studying Consolata, measuring her up. Some girls, at eleven or twelve, look strong—like they can carry the world on their backs. But not Consolata. She was a small girl.

Shayo turned to me and whispered, "Consolata can't carry me. I'm going to tell her to run. She can follow the crowd. Maybe she'll live."

I looked back out toward the road. It was terrifying out there. Black smoke and red light smothered the neighborhood. Some of the houses were on fire.

I knew what I had to do. I had to let Ma Muloko go with Consolata. Ma Muloko was stronger and older than Consolata. Together, they might survive. The moment had come. It was the moment I had been trying to escape all my life—the moment when everyone leaves.

Through our tears, we hugged each other goodbye. I begged Ma Muloko to run as fast as she could. "If you hear that the Centre burned, buy a ticket to Masisi and tell my mother that I died."

That was all I could think of—my mother. She had sacrificed everything to bring me to this place. And now I would die here. Everyone would shake their heads at my mother. They would click their tongues, and their voices would drip with pity. They would say how foolish she was—how she should have abandoned me a long time ago.

"Tell my mother I love her," I said as I let go of Ma Muloko's hand. She and Consolata turned toward the road. They ran, and we stayed behind.

Chapter 45

Shayo and I were alone at the Centre. We wheeled ourselves around the deserted grounds and stopped by the volleyball bench where we'd spent happier days. We could see the roofs of houses burning and orange flames shooting into the sky. Night was coming and, in the darkness, no one was going to save us.

We sat by the bench for a long time. After a while, I saw the silhouette of a man stumbling toward us through the smoky, red haze. Maybe it was someone coming to save us. But no. It was an old man with one leg, walking on crutches. The man hobbled over, his face full of horror. "Oh no, dear God! What are you still doing here?" he wailed. His head spun around. "You can't be here! I am old, but you are children."

Shayo and I sat in our wheelchairs and stared at the old man.

"Let me pray for you," he suggested. Without waiting for an answer, he pounded his crutches into the ground and raised his hands to the sky. After his prayer, the old man rushed off, thumping forward on his crutches. We were alone again, but his prayers stayed with us, and I didn't feel so alone anymore.

The gate of the Centre stood open. In the street we could see the shadows of people running—children getting lost, calling out to their parents, hands clutching each other, trying to hold families together.

Suddenly, through the thick smoke, I saw the shape of a man with his family. He was rushing toward our gate, and his family was trying to pull him back. He stopped and shook his head, then pointed for them to go on without him. He turned away from his family and back toward the Centre. This man was coming inside.

When the man ran through the open gate, I recognized him. It was Papa Katenge, the worker whose gentle voice had always encouraged me. He saw Shayo and me by the volley-ball bench and jumped in surprise. "Binti zangu! My daughters!" he cried, grabbing our hands and checking to see if we were whole. "What are you still doing here?"

We offered no answer.

"Well girls...this is a world of strange things, isn't it?" Papa Katenge stammered. He threw his eye across the compound and caught sight of the chapel. "Let's go to pray," he urged. "Only God can save his children."

Papa Katenge grabbed the back of Shayo's wheelchair and started to push her toward the chapel. By now, everything in the world was red, and when Shayo looked over at the chapel, her whole body straightened and leapt back. The chapel had red, stained-glass windows, and now the building glowed so fiercely that it looked like it was on fire.

As Papa Katenge pushed Shayo and her wheelchair past the volleyball net toward the chapel, Shayo grabbed hold of the pole that held up the net. The wheelchair jerked back in the dirt, nearly toppling over.

"I'm sorry, Papa, but I won't go to the chapel today," Shayo insisted. I'd never heard her voice so firm before. She was clutching the pole, shaking her head, and refusing to move. "God knows where we are. I'm not going in there."

Papa Katenge studied her in confusion. He let go of her wheelchair and came toward me. I grabbed the wheels of my wheelchair so that they refused to move. I loved that chapel, and I loved to pray. Around the Centre, people sometimes called me Pastor, but this was too much.

"Honestly, Papa! Today, we're not going to the chapel," I insisted.

Papa Katenge pressed his hands together and looked at us in our wheelchairs. His face was sad. "My God, what will I do?" he asked.

No one said anything.

Papa Katenge looked at us and spoke again. "Do you want me to try and take you out of here?" he asked doubtfully, nodding toward the gate. The streets were still crowded with people and choking with smoke. "We might die out there," Papa Katenge warned.

"We'll die for sure if we stay here!" I exclaimed before I could circle my tongue.

Papa Katenge nodded. He sprinted over to the offices where the men with polished shoes worked. After a few minutes, he came back with the key to one of the vans. My heart jumped. We were saved! We were going to leave! Papa Katenge plucked me out of my wheelchair and placed me in the passenger seat of the van. Then he ran back to pick up Shayo and put her next to me.

Papa Katenge was a man who liked to do everything slowly and carefully, but now his eyes looked wild as they jumped from one building to the next. He turned toward the dormitory. "Is anyone else in there?"

I remembered Papa Jules, and I nodded. Papa Katenge raced toward the dormitory, yelling. A voice echoed back, and Papa Katenge followed the voice into the building. When he emerged again, he was carrying a thin mattress. He opened the back doors of the van and threw the mattress on the metal floor. Then he rushed back into the building and returned with Papa Jules hoisted on his shoulder. Papa Katenge gently laid Papa Jules on the mattress in the back of the van and slammed the door shut. We were ready to go.

When Papa Katenge climbed into the driver's seat, he hesitated. The air was so thick with smoke that we could hardly see anything now. "I don't know if we'll live," Papa Katenge said, as he reached in his pocket for the key. His hand shot back out of his pocket, and he began patting his body. His eyes grew into wide circles. "I don't have the van key," he said.

Papa Katenge ran in every direction, searching frantically for the key. He ran back through all the buildings. When he returned, his hands were still empty. "The key is gone," Papa Katenge admitted, looking defeated. We nodded, because there was nothing more we could say.

A thought came to me. Papa Katenge had picked us up. Maybe the key had fallen when he leaned over.

"Check over by the volleyball bench," I suggested.

Papa Katenge flew out of the van and ran over to the bench. He fell to his knees, wildly patting the ground. Suddenly he clambered to his feet and ran back to the van with the key in his hand. We were saved again!

The engine roared, and Papa Katenge edged the van out of the Centre and into the road. It was impossible to know which way Papa Katenge would go. There were people everywhere. "I'll try to find the way to the border," Papa Katenge muttered to himself. But as soon as he started out the gate, he changed directions. "No, we can't leave the others," he murmured.

Just down the road was a second compound where the patients with quadriplegia lived. I visited those patients every week. The staff at the Centre were always telling us that we had to visit one another—to bring encouragement to those who suffered. Papa Katenge was headed into that compound now.

When we arrived, I saw that we weren't alone. This compound was still full. Nuns and priests were running frantically. They called for patients and loaded them into various vehicles. Papa Katenge climbed out of our van. Before he could say anything, the priests began piling patients into the back of our van, laying them first on the mattress and then flat on the metal floor, one on top of another. Papa Katenge hustled over to speak with some of the priests. When he returned to the van, he said we were going to join the caravan and follow the priests to another compound on the far side of Goma where we would be safe.

I don't remember the roads that we drove, but eventually we reached the priests' compound. Someone lifted me out of the van and set me on the grass. Shayo sat next to me. I looked around. Spread out on the grass were twenty or thirty men. The priests and Papa Katenge left us to rest in the grass and vanished into one of the buildings. They must have been making plans for where we would sleep.

Outside on the grass, I gulped in the air. It was cool, and it didn't stick in my throat. I thought maybe we had survived.

Suddenly, an explosion rocked the air. Everyone started screaming. "We're dying again!" we all wailed. The priests came running out of the building to see what was wrong. The tin roof from a building nearby had exploded from heat. Seeing that the fire had come close, the priests and nuns and Papa Katenge scrambled into action again. They hoisted everyone back into the vehicles. Papa Katenge grabbed Shayo and me and put us in the front seat again. Men were stacked, like sacks of corn, in the back of our vehicle. Someone slammed the door shut.

No one said where we were going or what we were doing. It was long past the time for talking. I didn't say anything. By that time, my heart had already left my body.

Papa Katenge returned to our van and started to drive. This time the road was empty. There were no people and no cars, only red sky and black smoke. I saw fire spilled out like honey on the ground.

We lurched to a stop. There were cars and motorcycles jamming the road in front of us. "We're near the border to Rwanda," Papa Katenge explained. People were abandoning their vehicles, climbing out and walking the rest of the way to the border.

Papa Katenge pressed his forehead onto the steering wheel and sighed. There was no way we could get out and walk. The men piled into the back of our van were silent. Their hearts must have left their bodies, too.

Papa Katenge tried to nudge our van forward between the cars. Suddenly, bullets started to cry. Someone was shooting. A soldier raced to Papa Katenge's window and banged on it. He had a gun pointed at Papa Katenge's face. "Where are you going?" the soldier shouted. "The border is closed for cars."

Papa Katenge raised his hands in the air. They were shaking.

"Get out!" the soldier exploded.

I was sitting in the front seat next to Shayo. I tried to shrink into her. Papa Katenge opened the door, and his feet dropped to the ground. I was afraid the soldier would shoot him. After a long silence, Papa Katenge's quiet voice emerged. "Do you see the name on this van?" he asked the soldier. I thought of the lettering on the side of our vehicle: *Centre Pour Handi-capés.*

The soldier stared at Papa Katenge. "Open up. Let me see what's in back," he demanded.

I heard Papa Katenge open the back door, and I twisted to see what was happening behind me. I saw something dripping off the edge of the back door. It looked red, but everything in the world looked red. Then I saw a mangled foot. Someone's foot had been slammed in the door, and no one had even noticed.

The soldier looked at the blood and the men lying in the van. He didn't say another word. He shut the door. Papa Katenge returned to the driver's seat, and the soldier waved us forward.

Chapter 46

After we crossed the border, we stopped again. We were surrounded by walls of people, cars, and motorcycles. The whole city of Goma had poured into the narrow village streets of Rwanda. Behind us, the sky still glowed fiery red. We were sticky and hot in the van, so we lowered the windows.

"Argentine, don't you have a song you can sing for us?" Papa Katenge asked. His voice pulled me back into my body, and I tried to think of a song. I always had songs in my head, but now the only thing I could think of was the red sky and the fire spilled out like honey. I thought of Papa Katenge spinning frantically around the deserted Centre. "This is a world of strange things," he had said. He was right. I started to sing.

"Mungu wetu wa ajabu, ajabu, ajabu." People passing our van stopped to listen to the singing. "Our God of wonders, wonders, wonders." They ran their fingers across the lettering on the side of our vehicle.

"Ehh! Centre Pour Handicapés! Ni ajabu kabisa!" They whistled. "It's a wonder indeed."

After what seemed like a long time, Papa Katenge started driving again. We reached a flat area, and Papa Katenge stopped the vehicle and hoisted us out, placing us on the grass nearby. Shayo and I unbuckled our leg braces and lay on the earth to rest our aching backs. Since we had no crutches and no wheelchairs, there was nowhere to go. We lay on that patch of grass and waited, unsure what would come next.

When morning came, the air was still heavy with smoke, but we could see the shape of a church in front of us. Behind us, a hill rose sharply. Nuns and priests were giving out cups of sugar water. There were far too many people to feed us all.

"What if the fire spreads to Rwanda?" a woman nearby murmured nervously.

"It can't reach us here," someone answered.

I hoped he was right. The day passed, and we didn't move. We were stuck on the ground, surrounded by exhausted people in every direction.

That night, the ground started to shake. Cries rose from the crowd.

"It's an earthquake! The earth will swallow us all!"

Some people started to run. I was scared we'd be trampled in the darkness. *We should have stayed at the Centre*, I thought. It would have been better to die in a place that we knew.

The shaking stopped and started all night. It was a terrible feeling. We were at the end of the world.

The next morning, a priest came to me and Shayo. "Papa Katenge told us you were here," he explained. "We have to go."

Go where? I wondered, but my heart had already left my body again, and I didn't have the energy to utter my question. The man placed us on the seats of a crowded minibus. As we started to move, I braced myself on the seat. My back felt weak as though I could barely hold myself up. The bus turned onto a curvy road, and we started to climb up the hill. With every turn in the road, the temperature seemed to fall. Our vehicle was climbing away from Goma—away from everything familiar. I knew I was going in the wrong direction.

All my life, Mama had told me to stay where she left me. *Don't go to the spring. Stay by the house. Don't come out until I return.* And every time that I failed to listen, I found myself lost and alone—stranded in the rain or lost in the streets of Goma.

Now, I was in a minibus that was carrying me farther and farther away from the Centre Pour Handicapés—the place Mama had left me. What would happen when Mama returned to Goma? How would she ever find me again? I'd be lost in another country with no way to return home. Mama would think I'd died in the eruption.

My thoughts were interrupted by the sound of a metal gate opening. Nuns and priests started unloading our vehicle, but I didn't want to get out. I didn't know where we were, and the air felt cold and unfamiliar. No one smiled. The nuns led us toward a building with rows of rooms. Each room had its own empty bed. This seemed strange to me. *Where are the people who sleep in these beds?* I wondered.

Days passed in that cold place. Every day, the priests brought more people, and I felt more lost. Until one day, I saw a face that I recognized. "There's Bunyere!" I cried. She was sitting in her metal kinga, next to Habimana and Joli. We threw ourselves into each other's arms, and we were home again.

Habimana told us how they had fled on Bunyere's kinga. I thought of the doctors shaking their heads dismissively at Bunyere, but maybe she had known what was best all along. That kinga had saved them. Habimana had piled Bunyere and Joli into the kinga and tied Joli's wheelchair behind. He had pushed the two girls in that heavy kinga through the panicked crowds and toward the border.

One by one, we started seeing more faces that we recognized, each with their own story. Someone told me how they had seen Papa Donatien on the road in Rwanda. He was strapped to his wife's back, and their baby was tied to her chest. They'd made it all the way to Rwanda like that.

But there were other people who no one had seen.

The days went by slowly, looking for faces we recognized. Consolata and Ma Muloko arrived. They were alive. We saw Papa Katenge again. "Binti zangu! My daughters!" he exclaimed as he looked at the way we were sprawled out on the ground. "Really girls, why are you sitting? You must practice standing!" he chided earnestly, and we smiled at his familiar admonishments and reminded him that we didn't have our crutches.

One day, the priests announced that they were sending a group back to Goma to see what remained of the Centre. They asked for volunteers, and Habimana offered to go. Before leaving, Habimana turned to Shayo and me. "What can I bring back from the Centre for you?"

I stared at Habimana. His question had no meaning. *What do you think you will find in Goma?* I wanted to ask. We had lost everything. The Centre had been lost—just like my home in Shahalia had been lost. It was a place I would never be able to return to.

That evening Habimana came back. "What did you see?" I asked.

"The cathedral is gone," Habimana confessed. I thought of the cathedral with its enormous blue roof and triangular shape. The cathedral was the biggest building I had ever seen, and it was right near the Centre. I knew then that everything was gone.

Habimana continued, "But the Centre is still there."

I couldn't understand his words. "Say it again," I begged. But no matter how many times Habimana repeated the news, I couldn't believe it.

Habimana stood and walked away. Soon, he returned. In his hands, he held our wooden crutches—the ones Shayo and I had left in our room by our neatly-tucked beds. I had never been so glad to see my crutches before.

I touched the smooth wood. "Mungu asifiwe. God be praised," was all I could say.

And then that song rose in my heart again.

"Mungu wetu wa ajabu, ajabu, ajabu."

"Our God of wonders, wonders, wonders."

Chapter 47

When Habimana gave us our crutches, he also brought more news from Goma. The city was covered with fire that had spilled on the ground like honey. It was called lava. Goma was already crowded with people returning home. People came back looking for lost family members and praying their houses hadn't caught fire. They returned to claim whatever they'd left behind, before someone else stole it away.

Habimana had seen Sister Aimée, one of the nuns from the Centre. The morning after the eruption, she had returned to the compound for patients with quadriplegia looking for those who might have been left behind. When she arrived, she saw paths of lava still burning hot. She heard a voice crying out, "I'm here. I'm still alive."

In one of the rooms, she found a man who was paralyzed. He was lying alone on a bed, hot and choking. There were streams of lava on both sides of the building, but somehow that man had survived.

We thanked God for the man who was saved, but not every story ended that way. There were others who died. Da Georgette, the woman who walked proudly through the kitchen at the Centre with her powdered face, red lips, and fine kikwembe—she died. She had been home on the day of the eruption, like all the other workers from the Centre. When her family realized what was happening, they put Da Georgette in her kinga and tried to push her to safety. But that kinga was no match for the lava and smoke and panicked crowds. Da Georgette never made it to safety.

We could only imagine how many other people with disabilities had disappeared that day. There were so many stories we'd never know. No one knew anything about an old man with one leg, the one who pounded his crutches on the ground and raised his hands to the sky to pray. I'd never seen him before the volcano erupted, and I never saw him again.

Eventually, after what could have been days or weeks in that cold, foggy place, the priests announced that it was time to return to the Centre. I was relieved but also scared—unsure of what we would find. When we returned, I saw the cathedral burned to the ground and the Centre nearby, still standing. There was no way to understand what had been taken and what remained.

I felt like I had when we returned to our house in Shahalia after my brother, Bonheur, died. I felt strangely exposed. Before the eruption, the Centre had felt like its own world, circled with a wall. I thought I could stay inside those walls forever. But now I was seeing how quickly walls disappeared and roofs melted. Even the houses of the wealthy had gone up in flames.

I no longer felt protected at the Centre. The big, shiny gate no longer looked like it could keep out the danger. All I had ever wanted was to find a place where I could feel safe. In Shahalia, when we'd heard gunfire, I had asked my mother if there was a place where bullets didn't cry. "Are there countries where people have peace?"

At the Centre, I thought I had found safety and peace. I had felt protected. Until one day, when the sun didn't shine, and all the people disappeared, and I found myself sitting alone and empty-handed again. It occurred to me now that I would never find anywhere safe in the whole world.

On the radio, we heard warnings not to drink the water that fell from the sky. They said it was dirty. But how could the water that cleanses us become dirty? And what else could we drink? The water pumps in Goma were dry, and everyone was thirsty.

Our neighbors started coming to visit the Centre again. Boys and girls who had played on the volleyball team arrived. Church groups returned on Sunday afternoons. These were the people who lived in those small wooden houses outside the Centre. It was the neighborhood where Mama and I had first stayed in the guest house, with its cramped rooms and the sharp bite of a pit latrine—the neighborhood I had been so eager to leave.

Now, here were our neighbors, visiting us again. I was thankful to see them. They wanted to know if we were safe. They shared stories about what had happened to them on the day the volcano erupted. I began to realize that they had suffered, too. They had struggled to carry children and old people. Their houses had burned.

As I listened to their stories, I realized that on the day the volcano erupted, there had been many people nearby. We just couldn't see each other through the smoke and the fire and the panic.

Chapter 48

I was beginning to learn a lesson that the Centre had been trying to teach me for years—a lesson about living in society—vivre en société.

Ever since I arrived at the Centre, the staff had been telling us to visit other people. Whenever I felt sorry for myself or overcome by the pain, the staff would ask, "Have you visited Papa Jules? Have you visited the compound for people with quadriplegia? We all must visit each other," they'd cluck.

That was the lesson they repeated over and over. No one is helpless. We can all bring encouragement to someone else.

When Mama and I arrived at the Centre, one of the first things we heard about was a celebration called Onze Onze. "Wait until you see Onze Onze," people would say. At first, I didn't understand that Onze Onze was a date in French— Eleven Eleven— November 11.

Soon, I learned that Onze Onze was a great holiday at the Centre. It was a celebration of Louis Martin, the Belgian doctor who founded the Centre. By the time we arrived in 2000, Louis Martin was no longer at the Centre. "It's too bad you didn't come when Martin was here," people were always telling me. They said that Louis Martin had been a very good man. He had carried people with disabilities on his own back. And even though Louis Martin was no longer at the Centre, the celebrations of Onze Onze continued.

On the day of Onze Onze, workers arrived at the Centre early and cooked big pots of food. People on kingas and crutches started to arrive. Everyone was invited: students from the physiotherapy school, nuns, priests, and people with disabilities from all around Goma. We sang, performed skits, and ate until our bellies were full. The lesson of every song and every skit was always the same—kushirika umoja—to join together.

On Onze Onze we not only celebrated inside the Centre, we also took our celebration outside, sending committees to visit the prisoners and the sick, just like the Bible instructed. Before the volcano erupted, I had never been part of those committees. My legs had been in plaster, and I had been unable to leave the Centre.

Still, I had always known there was a prison behind us. Sometimes we heard gunfire coming from that direction. The first time I heard those bullets, it scared me. I thought the war had followed me from Masisi to Goma, but my friends told me not to worry. "It's just prisoners trying to escape," they said.

After the volcano erupted, I began to see my neighbors in ways that I had never seen them before. I began to realize that our neighbors needed us as much as we needed them.

That brought my attention to the prisoners nearby. Weren't they our neighbors, too?

"What do they do in the prison?" I asked my friends.

"They suffer," someone answered. Those words clung to me. I knew what it meant to suffer.

That year, when the staff at the Centre asked for volunteers to visit the prisoners, I raised my hand. I was getting stronger on my crutches, and I wanted to find out what was happening inside that prison.

When we arrived at the prison, the guards studied our faces and wrote our names in a book. From inside, I could hear deep voices singing and clapping. It was so loud that it sounded like an army of men, and I began to grow nervous. I could feel my legs shaking.

Someone opened a door. I moved carefully on my crutches through a long, dim hallway. It was difficult to move, and I didn't want to fall. We arrived in a bare courtyard where men stood shoulder to shoulder. There was no shade from the sun or protection from rain.

"Karibu wageni," the men sang. "Welcome visitors."

I felt small and overwhelmed. I didn't belong in here with all these towering men.

The priests said a prayer and the prisoners formed a long line. When they reached the front of the line, each man held out his plate, and someone from our committee scooped food onto the plate. I stood by the side of the table to watch.

"Thank you, sister," the men said to me as they walked past.

My friends had explained to me that prisoners had to provide food for themselves. They counted on family and friends to visit and bring food. As I watched the prisoners march forward in the bare courtyard, I could see their lives on their faces. The prisoners who had visitors looked strong. I knew they had food to eat. The prisoners who had no one to visit them looked empty and haunted. I could see they were starving.

After we left the prison, I couldn't forget the hollow faces of those men who had no one to visit them. It made my stomach hurt.

That was the lesson of Onze Onze. We were all called to visit each other. No one, not even a prisoner, was meant to be walking alone.

Chapter 49

The next January, Bunyere told me she would be returning home for the July break. "Home?" I stammered. July was the month when the staff rested, and the Centre emptied out. Many of the older patients returned to their homes to visit their families. But we were teenage girls, and we'd grown up at the Centre with our legs in plaster. We usually stayed at the Centre even when others left. By the end of August, we'd be bored and anxious for everyone else to return.

Now, Bunyere was preparing to go home for the break, and I wanted to understand where she was going.

"Back to Kitchanga," she laughed.

I didn't know much about Kitchanga, but I knew it was a town on the road leading to Mweso. "What's it like there?" I asked.

"It's just home," Bunyere answered.

I wanted to see my family too, but I knew I'd never go home to Shahalia. It was too far away. How would I even get there? I had become a person who walked on two legs, crutches thumping beside me. When I thought of Shahalia, and the dirt path that turned to mud when it rained, I knew I'd never go home. In Shahalia, I had been a small girl, easy to carry. Now, I was bigger and heavier, with straight legs and metal leg braces. I could never return to Shahalia. What would happen if our neighbors pounded a wooden spoon on a pot like a drum, and my family stood to run? Would I say, "Wait for me," as I painstakingly buckled my leg braces? Would I teeter downhill on my crutches? I knew it wasn't possible. But now, as I watched Bunyere preparing to visit Kitchanga, I wondered nervously if one day the doctors might expect me to return home as well.

It wasn't long before I received an answer to that question. The following year, Papa Laloir started talking about sending me home for the break, like Bunyere. "You're walking on crutches now. It's only for two months," Papa Laloir insisted, trying to encourage me.

I didn't say anything in response. I was a person who needed help, and people who need help do what they're told.

I was instructed to send word to my mother, so she could start preparing for my visit. We still had six months. That would be plenty of time to prepare, Papa Laloir assured me.

A few months later, my mother arrived at the Centre. She brought news of my brothers and my father. My friend Bébé had gotten married.

After we discussed all the news from Shahalia, Mama and I tried to make plans. We both knew that going back to Shahalia was impossible for me.

"Where will I go?" I asked Mama.

"We'll move. We're your family. We have to move," she said.

Move? How could I ask my family to move? They didn't have any money, and even if they did, where would they go?

I thought of Kitchanga—the town where Bunyere's family lived. It was on the main road, where trucks and buses traveled. It was closer to Goma than Mweso. Bunyere had gone there on the break and returned to the Centre without any problems. This year she was leaving the Centre for good, returning to live with her parents in Kitchanga. If Bunyere could survive in Kitchanga, maybe I could too.

My mother left the Centre saying she would ask my father to move to Kitchanga. I thanked my mother, because I knew she was doing everything she could, but I also knew that my father would never agree to move. He was from the area surrounding Shahalia. He'd built our house by hand and tiled the roof. For him, life wasn't so bad in Shahalia. Why would he move to Kitchanga, where we had nothing?

Eventually, I received word from my family. My mother had given birth to a new baby, a girl named Aline. And my father had agreed to move to Kitchanga. This news terrified me. My family was moving to Kitchanga for me. The weight of it was heavy. My family was carrying me again.

"Don't be afraid. It's only for two months. You'll come back again soon..." the staff at the Centre repeated as the break grew near. But I didn't want to go to Kitchanga. I was terrified that I might never return to the Centre.

Chapter 50

On July 2, I walked out of the Centre with crutches under my arms and braces on my legs. "I'll be back soon," I promised everyone, including myself. I stepped cautiously into the road and checked for sand where my crutches might slip. Motorcycles sped by. There were people shouting and honking horns. I placed my crutches in front of me and threw my legs forward, praying I would land.

Goma had changed since the volcano erupted. It was barely recognizable. Houses were buried under lava rock. Some neighborhoods were sickeningly empty, covered in dark, hardened masses of earth. I thought of how Mama had described the rivers of Mweso vomiting water into the streets. This looked like the insides of the earth had been vomited up. If the streets had been rocky before, they were nearly impassable now. I called for a motorcycle taxi to take me to Birere, the crowded neighborhood where Mama and I had first arrived.

In Birere, I found a minibus headed to Kitchanga and hoisted myself inside. We wove through the crowded streets until the city became a blur behind us. On the edge of the city, white tents stretched into the distance. The woman sitting next to me said that these were the camps—full of villagers who couldn't go home.

Soon, the people in the minibus started to murmur.

"We're coming to the checkpoint in Sake."

"God help us through Sake."

When I asked what they meant, the woman next to me only shook her head and said, "Sake's a place you don't want to spend the night."

We reached the checkpoint in Sake, and our minibus jolted to a stop. Men with rifles hanging carelessly off their shoulders were standing outside a building. Our driver climbed out of the minibus.

"He'd better pay whatever they ask," the woman beside me said as she watched our driver follow the soldiers into a building.

"If they beat him, we'll all be stuck in Sake tonight," another passenger mumbled. I wished desperately that we had already arrived in Kitchanga. But I knew Sake was only the beginning of the journey.

Looking out the window, I could no longer see our driver or the men with guns and uniforms. Our minibus was surrounded by people knocking on our windows. They were selling bundles of cassava leaves, sugar cane, and roasted corn. The smell of the corn carried me back to my brothers. I thought of how Ushindi loved roasted corn, and I waved toward a woman with a basin on top of her head. I bought three cobs of corn and tucked them next to the bread from Goma—gifts for my family.

Our driver returned, and I studied the back of his head, wondering what kind of person did this dangerous job. We pulled away from the barrier, and soon we made a sharp turn, climbing away from the lake and into the steep hills on a road that twisted back and forth like a snake.

Soon, we arrived at a place where the road was so steep that the front of our minibus tilted upward sharply. Everyone in the vehicle leaned forward. I clung to the seat and prayed we wouldn't slip back down the road and over the ledge. Our tires spun in the slippery mud. The woman next to me started knocking on the metal ceiling of the minibus. Soon, everyone was knocking and yelling for the driver to stop.

"We won't make it! Let us out here! We'll walk up the hill," passengers shouted, and when the driver stopped, they all scrambled out.

I sat there in the tilting minibus, watching all the other passengers leave, until there was no one left but the driver and me. The driver looked back over his shoulder and shrugged at me, and we lurched forward again. I closed my heart. If we fell over the ledge, we'd never survive.

When we reached the top of the hill, the other passengers were waiting. They climbed back into the vehicle, and we continued our journey.

By the time we arrived in Kitchanga, it was late in the day. Darkness was coming, and we were all exhausted. I clambered out of the vehicle and steadied myself on my crutches, wondering what I would find in Kitchanga.

Chapter 51

When I arrived in Kitchanga, my whole family was standing by the side of the road. My parents, my four brothers, and a new baby girl were all waiting for me.

I hadn't seen my father, Tera, and Espoir since I left Shahalia three years earlier. The last time they'd seen me I was a small girl who crawled on the ground. Their eyes widened at the sight of me on my crutches. "It's her! She's standing!" Tera shouted as his narrow face broke into a wide smile. A crowd started to gather around us.

"Is this your girl? The one you told us about?" someone asked my father.

"Yes, this is my daughter," my father said. I couldn't believe that my father had told people about me.

"Let's go," Mama prompted.

I didn't know where we were going, but I hoped it wasn't far. The road was made of dirt and full of holes. When I placed my crutches on the ground in front of me, they slid in the sand. When I put my weight on them, they slipped out from under me. This wasn't like walking at the Centre on those smooth, cement walkways. I had to move slowly, tentatively placing each crutch on the ground and testing its sturdiness.

The crowd stood back and watched, narrating my every step as though I couldn't hear them.

"Look at that girl! She is standing on crutches!"

"My God, she can walk!"

"Yee! She's going to fall!"

My pace was painfully slow. Soon the crowd began to lose interest and peeled away. Children ran off to find a new game, and only my family continued walking slowly by my side, lifting me whenever I started to slip. I was already growing too tired to continue.

"Mama, how far away is our house?" I asked.

"Well...it's not too far," Mama answered hesitantly. "But it's still a ways..."

My legs, with their braces, had grown so heavy that I could barely swing them anymore. I scanned the side of the road, looking for a place where I could rest, but there was nowhere I could sit with my leg braces. Slowly, I continued thumping my way forward.

"Mama, how far is it now?" I repeated after what seemed to me like a long time. My hands were cramping, and I wasn't sure how much longer I could hold onto my crutches.

"See that tree in the distance? That's where we turn," Mama waggled her finger. I could see the tree. It didn't look too far away, so I tightened my grip on my crutches and started thumping again. More time passed. The sun was sinking low. Evening was coming, and I still hadn't even reached that tree.

Mama studied me sympathetically. "Can you continue just a little further?" she asked.

Relief rushed through me. *We're almost home,* I thought.

But then Mama continued. "Papa Léonard's house is right up the road. We can sleep there tonight, and we'll continue walking tomorrow."

Continue walking tomorrow? My hope was cut. I was exhausted. *Our house must be very far away,* I thought.

As evening fell, we arrived at Papa Léonard's house. "Welcome, chérie," Papa Léonard said as he led me into a room with a wooden bench and stools for sitting. I sat on the wooden bench and wished for somewhere to lean my back.

This was the first time I met Papa Léonard, but I had heard of him all my life. Years ago, before I was born, my grandfather and Papa Léonard had formed a sacred pact—igihango. They slit open their skin, drank each other's blood, and swore to treat each other's families as their own. Papa Léonard was Hunde, and my grandfather was Hutu—but their blood pact had endured, despite the war between Hutu and Hunde—the war that had driven us out of Mweso when I was five. It was a pact that was meant to continue from generation to generation.

By the time my family moved to Kitchanga, my father's father had died, but Papa Léonard was still honoring their sacred pact. When my family had arrived in Kitchanga with nothing, Papa Léonard had welcomed them, inviting them to build a hut on a parcel of land that he owned.

Sitting in that dimly lit room, Papa Léonard offered me an orange Fanta. I grabbed it eagerly. I was so thirsty. But then I thought, *what will happen if I drink this Fanta? Where will I find a latrine?* It was like that time in Shahalia, when Bebe and Magambo had carried me across the hills to sing with the choir. I was older now, and my legs were straight, but I still had the same problem. I wouldn't be able to reach the latrine. I swirled the Fanta in my mouth slowly and forced myself to swallow. I didn't take another sip.

"Now, what can I bring you to eat?" Papa Léonard asked. But the same question came back to my head. *How will I go to the latrine?* Every person with a disability knows this question. We abandon our thirst and our hunger to maintain our own dignity.

"I like sugar cane," I answered. I was no longer a child, but sugar cane is something you can chew without filling up.

I slept that night at Papa Léonard's house. Mama carried a basin like a chamber pot for me. The next day we started walking again, turning off the main road and following a narrow path. I was tired. My whole body hurt. I had never walked this far on crutches. But my family had sacrificed everything to come to Kitchanga, and I couldn't give up.

"We're almost there," Mama promised as she watched me slowly heaving myself forward. But when I looked ahead, I was horrified to discover a stream running across the path in front of us. It was a small stream. If I had been crawling, I could have splashed across it, but on crutches I knew I would slip and fall. I stood there, completely overwhelmed, unable to move even one step further.

Mama stood beside me, but she couldn't carry me now. I was too heavy and awkward with my leg braces and crutches, and Mama had baby Aline on her back. We both stood there looking at the stream, unsure what to do next.

A neighbor emerged from a house nearby. She must have been watching us. She looked at me softly. Mercy washed over her face. She wiped her hands on her kikwembe and moved toward me. "Enough of that. I'll carry you across."

I was not accustomed to people carrying me anymore. With my braces on, I was heavy, and my legs stuck out stiff like tree limbs. I wrapped my arms around the woman's neck, and she hunched forward, pulling me onto her back, my legs sticking out behind me. We crossed the stream and after a few minutes, she set me back down. I was so thankful for that woman.

Finally, we reached our house. It was a hut, made from sticks and dried leaves. The entrance was low to the ground.

I'd never be able to enter on my crutches. Nobody had realized all the things that would be difficult for me now.

My brothers came toward me. They were excited and wanted to pull me inside. But there was no way I could enter without lowering myself to the ground. I gave up my crutches and lay on my stomach in the dirt, so I could I pull myself through the doorway.

In the hut, my brothers were still full of excitement. They had built a small bed for me with a mat suspended between four sticks. I sat on the edge of the mat and took off my braces.

"Let us see your legs!" my brothers whispered. They had never seen my legs straight.

That night, we sat together on the ground, the heat from our bodies keeping out the cold air. I listened to the story of how my family had moved for me. They had walked the whole journey from Shahalia to Kitchanga, everyone carrying something. Mama had carried baby Aline. She was tiny and beautiful with eyes like Mama. But I was sorry to see her here in Kitchanga—where we had nothing but a hut made with sticks and leaves. Even the land underneath our house was borrowed from Papa Léonard.

I couldn't stop thinking of our house in Shahalia with the tree that dropped fat avocados onto the ground. In Shahalia, we might have lacked oil and salt, but there had always been something to eat—blood fruit or bananas turning ripe outside our door. Now my family was living in Kitchanga where nothing came easy—and even the avocados cost fifty francs. It saddened me to hear that my brothers weren't going to school. Instead, they were hiking all the way back to Shahalia to harvest cassava greens from our fields so that we would have something to eat. What had I done to my family?

It rained nearly every day in Kitchanga. I only left our house a few times a week. I would crawl outside, and put on my leg braces, only to discover that I had nowhere to go. Our house was far from the main road. I could only sit in the sun, watching people walk by, just as I had in Shahalia.

On Sundays, I became determined to leave our house. Sunday was visiting day at the Centre, and even here in Kitchanga, that was important to me. We have to visit each other—it gives us strength to go on.

I had one friend to visit in Kitchanga: Bunyere. I hadn't seen her since she left the Centre, but I knew she was living with her parents and brother on the other side of Kitchanga. My mind whirled thinking about how I could visit Bunyere. I couldn't walk to her house on my crutches. It was too far away. I remembered Bunyere's kinga—the one she had wheeled happily around the Centre. She had brought that kinga to Kitchanga. I could send my brothers to borrow her kinga. It was like borrowing legs. I'd be able to go anywhere if I had her kinga.

I sent my brothers to find Bunyere's house, and they returned with her kinga. Bunyere's brother accompanied them. I was so happy to see the kinga that I didn't stop to wonder why so many boys might be needed. I climbed happily onto the seat.

"Tugende!" I exclaimed. "Let's go!"

At first, the boys pushed me forward without any problems. But soon we turned onto a narrow path and started uphill. One of the back wheels fell in a hole, and the kinga tilted sharply. I was stuck in a ditch. The kinga refused to move. These paths were not made for kingas. I thought about how easily Bunyere wheeled around the Centre.

That's when I understood. Bunyere had not moved to Kitchanga because it was a good place for people like us. She had moved here because there was no other choice.

The boys strained. Their bodies slanted sideways as they pushed at the kinga. I sat waiting. Finally, the kinga jolted out of the ditch and rolled forward again. But when we arrived at Bunyere's house, I realized that her kinga couldn't fit through the doorway. Sadly, I left the kinga behind and rose on my crutches to enter the house.

When my eyes adjusted to the dark house, I found Bunyere in bed. She was lying in bed because there was no place for her to sit. Her kinga was stuck outside. There were no chairs in the room. There was only a bench and a low stool, nothing to support Bunyere's wobbly back. In the corner of the room, I spotted Bunyere's sewing machine—untouched.

After visiting Bunyere, I returned to our house with my heart full of questions. This was not what I'd wanted. I had dreamed of learning to walk and coming back to my family like someone returning from the market carrying salt and oil.

But now I was sitting in Kitchanga with my mother carrying a basin like a chamber pot, while she also took care of my new baby sister.

What kind of future was there for me in Kitchanga—what kind of future was there for any of us?

Chapter 52

My time in Kitchanga passed slowly, and I began to wonder how I would return to the Centre. The staff had given specific instructions.

"Don't return empty-handed," they had said.

Every patient was expected to return with a family member and with money to contribute to the cost-of-living expenses. "You can't abandon your children here," the staff often warned families.

Now that I was sitting in our hut in Kitchanga, I saw that my family had nothing for me to bring back to the Centre. Mama had said she'd accompany me on the journey, but we didn't even have money for two bus tickets back to Goma.

"Don't be afraid. God will help us. We'll find more money," Mama said. Then, she started walking. She walked to my grandmother's house in Nyanzale and my grandfather's church on the farm. She visited my uncles, my aunts, my cousins, our church, and our neighbors. She came home with a bag of flour, a container of oil, and a stack of francs tucked into her clothes.

Mama sold the container of oil and added more francs to her collection, but still it wasn't much. She bought two bus tickets to Goma, and nearly all the francs disappeared. "God will help us," Mama repeated, as she tied Aline onto her back. We climbed on a crowded minibus headed for Goma. When we arrived at the Centre, we had only a sack of flour and a few, carefully folded five-hundred-franc notes remaining.

"This is all we have," Mama told the staff at the Centre.

They looked at us in horror. "Is this what you think it takes to feed your daughter for a whole year? This won't cover a week."

Mama fell to her knees, and I stood on my crutches nearby. "Have mercy on us," she begged.

I felt sorry to see my mother on her knees. What more could we offer? We had already given everything we had.

Finally, the staff agreed to take me back. By this time, I no longer needed a caregiver, so they sent Mama home to Kitchanga with sharp warnings to bring more food soon. Mama promised she would. But I knew it would be a long time before I saw her again.

When Mama left, I looked around the Centre. I was grateful to be back, but I knew it wouldn't last long. I had to prepare for whatever was coming next.

I became more determined than ever to practice walking. I wanted to be faster and stronger on my crutches. I didn't want to be afraid of falling. I circled the grounds of the Centre, thumping on my crutches and swinging my legs forward.

Memories of Kitchanga followed me. My family had moved there for me, and now they were suffering. I couldn't stay at the Centre forever, but I also couldn't return to my family in Kitchanga with nothing to offer. I needed a way to provide for my family.

There was a sewing program at the Centre. An instructor told me that if I joined the program, I might be able to learn to sew and provide for my family. In my head, I could still see Bunyere's abandoned sewing machine. I didn't know if anyone could support themselves by sewing, but I knew I had to try.

In sewing class, the teacher was strict, and her instructions were complicated. "Fold the fabric here. Iron the crease. Sew it like this," she said quickly.

"Yes, teacher," I answered earnestly. I carefully folded my fabric and carried it over to the ironing table, but the class was full of girls, all waiting to use one iron. By the time I reached the front of the line and ironed my fabric, I couldn't remember the rest of the teacher's instructions.

"Teacher, what did you tell me to do next?"

"Argentine, your head forgets very fast!" The teacher sighed. "Don't you understand that this work can help feed your family?"

She didn't need to say that. Every girl in the room was already desperately trying to learn to sew, and we all dreamed of taking care of our families.

I learned to sew baby clothes and men's shirts. The teacher told us to buy material so we could practice our sewing, but I didn't have money for material. I barely had money for soap and oil for my skin. For those things, I lived on the mercy of others. And there was always mercy. When people from the surrounding neighborhood came to visit, they sometimes tucked a hundred francs in my hands. With those francs I bought myself oil and soap. Sometimes I bought a mandazi to eat.

The electrician who worked at the Centre came to visit me as well. I had first met him when Magambo had been my caregiver. There were wires all over the Centre and, one time, Magambo had taken a shortcut in the rain and touched a wire behind a building. The electricity shocked her. Ever since then, the electrician would greet me with warnings to be careful of the wires.

When I told my electrician friend that my family had moved to Kitchanga, he looked at me in surprise. "They must really love you," he said, and he gave me money to help build a house in Kitchanga.

Still, I didn't have any money to buy fabric to practice my sewing, and I was afraid I'd never learn without practicing.

One day Papa Ruzi came to see me. He worked in partnership with the Centre, visiting rural villages and looking for children with disabilities who needed help. He was like a father to many people at the Centre, and he'd always been kind to me.

"Argentine, I need a shirt," Papa Ruzi said.

"Oh yes! Let me sew you a shirt," I replied enthusiastically as Papa Ruzi gave me money for the material. My friends and I went to Virunga market to buy fabric for Papa Ruzi's shirt.

I'd been to Virunga Market before, but I'd stayed at the tables on the edge of the market. Inside, the market was full of narrow rows that I didn't think I could navigate on my crutches. I was sure I would slip on the patches of sand. But now my desire to sew a shirt for Papa Ruzi was greater than my fear of falling.

I bought some fabric and sewed a shirt for Papa Ruzi. It must have been a little crooked because I wasn't very good at sewing yet. But Papa Ruzi accepted the shirt enthusiastically, and I saw him wear it one time. I was proud. I had never imagined that one day I'd become a person who sewed for a man like Papa Ruzi.

Chapter 53

Just as I was starting to progress in my sewing, a new problem arrived. I was walking past the offices one day, when one of the social workers called me over. "I want to see you in my office," he said.

I didn't want to go to that office. I'd always known that I didn't belong in those rooms with desks and men with polished shoes. I sat gingerly on the edge of the chair. The social worker looked at me and heaved a sigh. "Argentine, do you know where your mother is?"

I lowered my eyes and shook my head. It had been many months since Mama had returned to Kitchanga, and I hadn't heard anything from her. People said things in Masisi were bad.

The social worker sighed. "Argentine, you must leave. We don't have a sponsor for you anymore."

I stared at the man's polished shoes. *Leave? What happened to Sister Louise? Didn't she pay for my treatment?*

The man explained that my treatment was finished. I was in the sewing school now, and Sister Louise couldn't continue to sponsor me.

I didn't know anything about how money worked at the Centre. I'd never asked about it.

"We'll keep looking for another sponsor for you. If we find someone, you can come back," the social worker promised.

On the desk in front of him were files and notebooks and machines whose names I didn't know. I sat silently. There was nothing to say. For the poor, the rain is always falling, and no one asks why.

"Where will you go?" the social worker asked.

Mama's face flashed in front of my eyes. I wanted Mama. I wanted the touch of her skin—the smell of oil and soap and smoke from the fire. I wanted to go back to my family.

But as I opened my mouth to respond, another thought came to my head. I remembered the way Mama had carried my chamber pot in Kitchanga. How could I go back to my family empty-handed—with no kinga and no sewing machine and no future?

I straightened my shoulders and focused on the social worker. He was still talking, and I tried to listen. "If we find a new sponsor, we'll send for you," he promised again.

I knew if I went back to Kitchanga, no one was ever going to send for me. It was too far away, and the road was too dangerous. The staff at the Centre would forget about me. I'd be lost in Kitchanga forever.

I couldn't go back. I couldn't do that to Mama. She'd worked so hard to carry me to the Centre. Not once, not twice, but three times, she had carried me to the Centre.

"Argentine, can you stay in Goma? Do you have any family here?" the social worker asked.

"I have no one," I answered, giving the answer that Mama and I had repeated so many times. I knew it was true. I'd be thrown out of the Centre and into the streets of Goma, and I would be lost and alone.

But no one walks alone.

That's what the Centre taught us.

I stopped and thought again. Where could I go?

I thought of a neighborhood blazing with heat, where even the rocks burned my hands. I thought of a small brown house crowded with children.

"Argentine, you are welcome here anytime," Mama Pastor had said when we first arrived in Goma all those years ago.

I didn't know if Church Mahanaime was still standing, or if Pastor Amani and his wife were still living in that wooden house with their many children. But I was beginning to realize that my life was full of people—even when I couldn't see them. It was like the time when Mama hid my brothers and me on the hill called Gapfura. She hid each of us under a separate bush, but we were still all there together.

Across the desk, the social worker peered at me.

"Do you have anyone in Goma?" he asked.

"Yes," I answered.

And for the first time, I knew it was true.

Chapter 54

The poor don't arrive at the doors of the wealthy, asking for help from those who can afford it. We arrive at the doors of our neighbors—the people we know—the ones who have little more than ourselves.

I was headed back to Church Mahanaime, looking for Pastor Amani and his wife. I didn't even know if the church still existed. So much of Goma had changed after the eruption. The cathedral, the biggest church in Goma, had burned. All I could do was hope that Pastor Amani's small church had survived.

My friend, Denise, offered to accompany me. Denise had grown strong in the years since I had first visited her in the hospital with her shattered leg suspended above her. She could walk with a cane now. She offered to carry my one bag.

"How will you survive outside the Centre?" Denise asked, looking at the way I still wobbled tentatively on crutches. "What if we can't find the church? What if they don't take you in?"

My body felt empty. I remembered all the questions I had asked Mama when we first arrived in Goma. *Where are we going? Who will show us the way?* I understood now why Mama hadn't answered. Sometimes there are no answers.

Denise and I rode in a bus to the neighborhood of Katindo. Outside the window, I could see houses crowding into each other. When we climbed down from the bus, I saw a sign for

Church Mahanaime. It was still there. God had answered my prayer.

To arrive at a church in Africa is to know you will find someone there. We entered the building and found women praying inside. I sat on a bench in the back, as Denise prepared to leave. She was my last connection to the Centre. I grabbed at her hand. "If they find a sponsor for me, come and tell me," I begged my friend, and she promised she would.

After Denise left, I sat at the back of the church and waited. I was more alone than I'd ever been in my life. Except, I wasn't alone. Up front, I could see heads bowed in prayer. When the prayer ended, a woman looked up. It was Mama Pastor.

"Argentine, is that you?" she asked.

"It's me, Mama Pastor," I said. Then I threw myself on her mercy and confessed that I had no place to go.

Mama Pastor looked at me kindly. She didn't look surprised. She took me to her house. It was the same house I had visited years ago when Mama and I had first arrived in Goma. Mama Pastor had ten children, although a few had married and only seven were living at home at the time. I sat with Mama Pastor on the wooden frame of a couch. We passed the time talking, until we heard Pastor Amani coming through the door. My thoughts jumped. *What if he refuses me? What debt does he owe me?* It had been years since my father had known Pastor Amani and now, I had arrived, helpless, at his door again.

When Mama Pastor walked out of the room to greet her husband, I listened nervously to their voices. "We have a guest," she told him. "It's Sister Argentine." There was silence. I heard Mama Pastor's voice again, "Have you forgotten Argentine?"

Suddenly, Pastor Amani ducked through the doorway and stretched out his hand. "Sister Argentine," he said, smiling. "You are very welcome here."

Pastor Amani called to his children, and we all sat together, crowding into their small living room where the floor was made of rough pebbles of hardened lava.

"This is Argentine," Mama Pastor said to her children. "She is your sister now."

Chapter 55

That night I slept with the other girls in the family. I could see the way they pushed closer together to make room for me, and I woke desperately trying to think of how I could repay Mama Pastor and her family. If only I had something to offer.

In the cooking hut outside of their house, I found a pile of dishes. *Here is something I can do*, I thought, tucking my crutches under my arms. I knew how to wash dishes. I'd washed dishes in Shahalia and at the Centre. But, in Shahalia, I had been sitting comfortably on a stool, and, at the Centre, I'd been sitting in a wheelchair. Now, I was teetering on crutches with uneven pebbles of lava beneath me.

I lifted the jug of water above the basin. The weight of the jug shifted back and forth, and I nearly lost my balance. Water sloshed into the plastic basin and spilled onto the rocky ground. I tried to continue scrubbing the dishes, but by the time I had finished, there was water all over. I tried to put some of the dishes away, but I dropped a clay cup, and it shattered. I couldn't do anything. All my confidence from the Centre evaporated. I had nothing to offer anyone here.

And I had other problems. The bathroom at Pastor Amani's house was a pit latrine built on top of a mountain of rocks. The first time I saw it, I blinked my eyes, unable to understand why anyone would have piled rocks into a mountain behind their house. It was only later that I learned that many pit latrines in Goma were poised precariously on top of large piles of rocks. Mama Pastor explained to me that the ground in Goma was so full of lava rock that it was difficult to dig down far enough for the pit. So instead of digging down, they raised the latrines up.

The first time I saw the construction, I stood there behind Pastor Amani's house unwilling to move, promising myself that I would never drink anything again. There was no way I could climb the mountain of rocks with my crutches and braces, so I lowered myself to the dirt and unbuckled my leg braces. I was crawling again. I had returned to the place where I had started.

I wanted so much to be a good guest. And my mind was always turning, looking for something I could offer this family. Slowly, I learned how to be helpful. I asked Mama Pastor's son to carry the dishes outside in a basin for me before he left for school. Then, I sat on a small stool and washed the dishes just as I had back in Shahalia.

When Mama Pastor was home, I followed her around the house, asking for something to do.

"Oh? Do you think you can help?" Mama Pastor asked, unsure at first. But soon she learned my hands could be helpful. One day, Mama Pastor brought a pile of cassava branches home from the market. She handed them to me. "You said you wanted some work," she laughed. I seized on the branches eagerly, just as I had long ago in Aunt Kampire's house. I knew how to pluck cassava leaves.

On Sunday afternoons, Denise sometimes came to Pastor Amani's house to visit me. I would welcome her into the living room. "It's so quiet at the Centre without you," Denise would say. "We miss your noise."

In between Denise's visits, I tried not to think about the Centre—about who I had been and how I had imagined my future. Pastor Amani and his family were so kind, but I felt lost in a darkness that I couldn't escape. Months and months passed with me trying to think of nothing at all, trying only to wash the dishes and pluck cassava leaves.

One day Denise arrived while I was sitting outside. "You've really grown used to this life," she joked, looking at my stack of freshly washed dishes. I stood on my crutches and invited her inside, but before Denise even sat, she demanded, "Don't you notice anything?" Denise was still walking with her cane and wearing a long skirt. I didn't notice anything.

She widened her eyes. "Have you forgotten what day it is?" After a few breaths, she announced, "It's not Sunday today!"

She was right! It was the middle of the week, and patients at the Centre weren't usually given permission to visit friends in the middle of the week. That was for Sundays. I suddenly wondered why Denise was standing in Mama Pastor's living room in the middle of the week.

Denise's face cracked into a smile. "They've sent me! They want you to come back to the Centre!"

I shook my head, thinking she was only teasing me. "No! I don't believe you. Swear it!"

She drew her fingers across her neck and snapped them together. "Haki ya Mungu," she swore.

"Swear it again!" I squealed.

We broke into laughter, and soon we were making so much noise that Mama Pastor came rushing into the room. When she saw the joy on my face, she joked, "Don't tell me! Are they going to take my girl away?"

I smiled back at Mama Pastor, but then a terrible thought entered my head. I turned to Denise. "Wait. What did they say? Tell me the exact words."

"They want you to come to the office," Denise answered, but then she lowered her voice. "They said don't come alone."

My heart left my stomach as Denise explained that I had to return with a parent or whoever was caring for me.

Mama Pastor's eyes widened, and she stared at her hands. "What do they want from me? I have no money to pay to the Centre."

I lowered my head, embarrassed. How could they ask this of Mama Pastor? This was the reason my aunt and uncle had never visited me at the Centre. They didn't want to be responsible for my care. Mama Pastor wasn't even my family.

"You don't have to take me," I said quickly. "I'll find my mother. I'll send word to Kitchanga."

I hadn't seen my mother in a long time. But I couldn't bear to ask anything more from Mama Pastor.

Mama Pastor drew herself up. "No, my child. There is no time for Kitchanga. I'll go with you."

Chapter 56

When we arrived at the Centre, Papa Laloir came lilting over with his face lit up. "Argentine! You've made it back," he exclaimed. He glanced at Mama Pastor and raised his eyebrows. "This isn't your mother," he said.

I swallowed. I wanted desperately for the Centre to take me back, but I knew that I didn't have anything to offer them and neither did Mama Pastor. I thought of the time Mama and I had returned from Kitchanga with francs and a sack of flour. The staff had exploded. Now, Mama Pastor and I were arriving with nothing at all.

We waited nervously in front of the offices. I saw Joli across the courtyard, and she waved at me. Word spread, and my other friends came peeking. Everyone knew I was back, but no one knew if they were going to let me stay.

Someone called Mama Pastor and me into the office. No one was smiling. The man behind the desk smelled of cigarettes. He glared at Mama Pastor. "Who are you?" he asked, and before she could explain, he demanded, "Where is Argentine's mother?"

"Look—we all know the state of things in Masisi," Mama Pastor said gently.

The man behind the desk hesitated and shifted the conversation, "And what has Argentine been doing in your house?"

Mama Pastor's face brightened. "Oh, she is a very good girl. She washes dishes and helps me cook and cares for..." The man behind the desk waved Mama Pastor into silence as he turned to me.

"You can stay. But you must do one thing. Send word to Kitchanga. Don't let this year finish without your mother arriving."

Chapter 57

On my first evening back at the Centre, my friends and I walked to our rooms. Our laughter spilled into the night air as we crossed the grounds of the Centre. We were no longer assigned to the Salle des Malades, the room for sick people. Now we were living in a separate building next to the physical therapy school. We had grown up.

"How did you live out there between all those rocks?" my friends asked me in hushed voices.

I was happy to be back at the Centre with its smooth walkways. During the day, I talked and laughed with my friends. We watched volleyball games. I sang in the choir. I visited other patients who needed more help than me. As the year passed, I grew more confident on my crutches and stronger on the sewing machine.

But at night, my mind spun in circles, trying to plan for a future that was still covered in mist. I knew who I was at the Centre, but I was terrified of having to leave again.

Within a year, the staff told me it was time for me to graduate. I'd have to leave the Centre again and, this time, I'd return to my family in Kitchanga. I knew I would receive a sewing machine at graduation. They'd even give me some pieces of kitenge fabric. But I'd seen how much good that sewing machine and fabric had done for Bunyere in Kitchanga.

In class, the teacher told us to prepare for a final sewing evaluation. She explained that we had to sew and present trousers and a blouse. We could sew the blouse to fit our own body, but, for the trousers, we had to look for a customer. We'd be responsible for measuring the customer and sewing the trousers. On the day of the evaluation, the customer would wear those trousers like a fashion model, and our work would be judged.

I found a student from the physical therapy program who agreed to be my customer. He came to the sewing room, and I took out my measuring tape. I measured his legs and his waist as the teacher watched. She raised her eyebrows and silently wrote on a clipboard. When my customer left, I spread out my material and drew a pattern in chalk.

The teacher came over and looked at my work. "Are you sure that's right?" she asked. I looked at her warily. "If you're sure, go ahead and cut," she continued.

"Really? But do you think this is right?" I asked, hoping she might give me some help.

She said nothing. I cut the cloth, praying my measurements were correct.

The day for the evaluation arrived and we all waited nervously outside the sewing room. I was called inside. The large room was filled with humming voices and bustling people. Atelier owners from across Goma had come to judge our work. They held up my blouse and trousers and studied the stitching. They leaned on the desks and wrote on their papers. Next, they called for my customer. He left and came back wearing the trousers. I watched as he paraded in a circle in front of the judges. He bent over. He stood up. The judges inspected him carefully.

"Now it is your turn," one of the judges said to me. "Won't you wear the blouse that you sewed?"

I looked down, mortified. I did not want to model my blouse. I wasn't embarrassed of my sewing. I was embarrassed of my body. I knew the blouse fit. But it fit in the way that everything fit me. My back was crooked, and it would make my blouse look crooked. No matter how far I traveled, I couldn't escape my own body.

There was a long silence. At last, the teacher softened. "We've seen enough," she said. Then she called for the next student.

I knew it would be two days until the results were announced. In the middle of all the waiting, another instructor passed by me in the courtyard. "Don't worry Argentine, you've passed!" she whispered generously. Then she listed the names of my friends. We'd all passed.

As soon as the terror of the sewing evaluation ended, a new terror began. Graduation. There was no way to avoid it now. I'd be leaving the Centre soon. The staff called me into the office. "Send word to your family," they said. "You're going home," they announced.

But where is home? I wondered. I was like a bird who builds its nest by the side of the path. The wind will come, and the wind will blow. If that nest will stand, nobody knows.

I started saying goodbye to everyone at the Centre. I thanked all my teachers and doctors. I even knocked on the doors of the offices and thanked the men behind the desks.

"Are you really going back to Kitchanga?" people asked. I told them I was. They looked at me anxiously. But I was anxious too. I was thinking about whether I could start an atelier in Kitchanga, and whether my parents were still living in a hut made of leaves. I didn't stop to think about why the name of Kitchanga was making everyone nervous. I hadn't followed the peace accords in 2003 or the way the accords began to collapse in 2004. To me, war was something that had always existed, just like the rain.

"I'm going back to Kitchanga," I said. And I never asked why everyone looked so nervous.

Part III

LOVE

Chapter 58

I graduated from the Centre in January of 2006 when I was seventeen years old. My family sent word that my father would come to escort me home to Kitchanga with my new sewing machine and my new kinga. It was the first time—the only time—my father came to the Centre. He loaded my sewing machine and my bag into the back of the kinga that Papa Ruzi had given me. It was time to go.

In Birere, I used money that friends had given me to buy bread, sugar, and a bag of candy to bring to my family. We found a truck leaving for Kitchanga. The trucks going in that direction were less crowded. Strong men loaded my kinga into the back of the truck and lifted me up. I was leaving Goma the way I had come.

Our truck rumbled out of the city. My body swayed, and I tried to catch my balance. I was no longer a child who could cling to the strangers next to me.

When we reached Sake, our truck stopped. I peered over the edge and saw soldiers escorting our driver into a building.

When we started moving again, one of the other passengers pointed at the swampy water nearby. "If they kill you in Sake, no one will ever find your body," she said.

As we climbed into the curvy hills, I began thinking about what was waiting for me in Kitchanga. I thought of Bunyere, lying in bed with her sewing machine sitting uselessly in the corner. Could I really start an atelier in Kitchanga?

As we neared Kitchanga, our truck stopped again. There was a rope strung across the road. There were men with uniforms and guns. They looked hungry just like the soldiers in Sake, but eventually they waved us through.

It was almost dark by the time we arrived in Kitchanga. Mama was waiting by the side of the road with my siblings. "Sister has come home!" my brothers shouted happily, and I was thrilled to be back with my family.

"Wait until you see the place we built for you," fifteen-year-old Tera whispered. I knew my father had sold one of our fields in Shahalia and bought a small piece of land in Kitchanga. They'd built a new house on it with the money that my electrician friend had given us.

I rolled down the streets of Kitchanga in my kinga, and I felt proud to be home. Tera reported excitedly how he'd built a small hut for me.

"Sister, the door is big enough to walk in on your crutches," Espoir enthused.

When we reached the house, I couldn't see anything in the dark, only my brothers' faces as they gathered around me. I called Espoir and whispered for him to bring my bag. Out of the bag, I pulled a loaf of bread.

"God be praised! Is that Goma bread?" Mama cried. In Kitchanga, everything from the city of Goma was special.

"I brought tea and sugar," I announced proudly, holding up more plastic bags. My brothers and I smiled at each other. Then we begged Mama to make tea, and we sat there dipping Goma bread into our plastic mugs of sugary tea.

"Let's show her the hut," Espoir said, his voice full of excitement, taking me over to a small construction on the side of the house. "We can put your sewing machine on the table right there, and you can sleep over here," he explained.

I lay on a mat, and my brothers lay beside me. We were together again.

"One day maybe you'll take me to Goma," Espoir whispered.

"And me," Tera said.

"And me," Ushindi and Soleil echoed.

I closed my eyes, listening to the sound of my brothers breathing. Then I went to sleep dreaming of all the ways I would help them.

Chapter 59

When I awoke the next day, my brothers were standing outside with their friends. "This is our sister. She came back," they said. I still had my bag of candy from Goma, and I gave a piece of candy to every child who came to visit. Soon, all the children in the neighborhood were visiting me. "She's the one who gives out the candy," I heard them whisper, and I smiled, pleased to be the one who brought home the sugar.

I wanted that bag of candy to last forever, but I knew it would finish soon, and I was anxious to start sewing. My brothers carried my sewing machine outside so I could sew in the sunlight. With the fabric that the staff at the Centre had given me, I sewed shirts, and we hung those shirts on the bushes nearby, like a sign. It was just like the time I sold mutobe out of our house in Shahalia.

The only problem was that our house was far from the main road. Not many people passed by. I took whatever work I could get. I sewed shirts or hemmed pants for neighbors, even if they could only pay me a couple hundred francs.

After some time, a woman named Mbale came to our house and found me sewing. She had one good leg and hopped with a cane.

"I've heard of you," she said to me.

"What do you do in Kitchanga?" I asked, wanting to know how a woman like me was making a living in this place. But she shook her head and told me she didn't do anything.

Soon, I learned that Mbale knew how to sew, and we started sewing together in front of my house. But every morning, I watched nervously as Mama left for the fields. Sometimes she hiked to the fields alone, and I worried about her. I heard that in the fields around Kitchanga, soldiers found women alone and fell on top of them, taking what they wanted.

I begged my mother to stay close to the house—to never go to the fields on her own. I counted my money each day, knowing that if I had earned one thousand francs, it would be enough for our family to eat, and Mama could stay home the next day.

But soon I realized that hemming pants in front of our house with Mbale was never going to be enough to feed my family every day. I needed to sew on the main road, where customers could see me. I started saving my money to build a small atelier. Five hundred francs bought ten nails. One thousand francs bought a piece of wood. I counted by each nail and each piece of wood until I had enough to build a small shack, minus the roof.

A friend offered to rent a small piece of land for me on the main road. It was a corner of someone else's property. Still, I needed the tin for the roof. At our church, I'd heard they were dismantling an old building, so I went to the pastor to ask if he might give me some of the metal roof.

"I can only give you six pieces," he said.

"That will be enough," I answered. I was happy for even one piece.

A few months later, I paid some boys to build my small atelier on the main road. Mbale joined me there, and we sat by the main road sewing and greeting people as they walked by.

Now that I was sitting on the main road, I could see all the people in Kitchanga. Women walked down from the hills with milk to sell. They invited me to their church high in the hills. Soldiers walked through town wearing green and brown uniforms. I hated their uniforms and boots and guns. But I tried to be friendly with everyone. Children passed by looking for candy. Bunyere sometimes came to visit. Even though she didn't sew, we sang in a youth choir together.

All week, sitting at my atelier, I prepared for Sunday—visiting day. I invited everyone to come to our house, arranging one visitor after another. When Sunday came, my father would look at the line of visitors and shake his head. "Where do you get all these people?" he'd ask and laugh about how I could meet so many people without even standing up. All my life, I'd been learning to pull people toward me.

I was sewing and making friends, but soon I realized it still wasn't enough. My mother was still trudging off to the fields.

As I sat outside the atelier watching people walk by, it reminded me of how I used to sit outside our house in Shahalia, watching our dirt path fill with people on the way to the market. I saw men pushing chukudus and girls carrying bundles of cassava branches. But this time I saw it differently.

I saw those people on the way to the market, and I thought, *I can do that.* Then I thought about the candy and tea and bread I'd brought from Goma. I knew how much everyone liked everything that came from Goma. And I knew how to go to the market. My mind jumped with ideas.

I didn't have much money, only enough for one ticket to Goma. *It will have to be enough,* I thought. I woke up early the next morning and climbed onto a minibus back to the city of Goma. As we passed through Sake, I bought a bundle of fresh cassava leaves to bring to my friends at the Centre. I didn't have much to offer my friends, but everyone likes sombe, and no visitor should arrive empty-handed.

At the Centre, I greeted everyone. When people heard I'd come from Kitchanga, they raised their eyebrows and exclaimed "Mungu we!" Some people shook their heads and muttered, "You must be a child of Nkunda."

"Nkunda? Who is that?" I did my best to answer with wide eyes and a blank face. People said General Nkunda was a rebel who lived in the hills surrounding Kitchanga. But I knew it would do me no good to talk of such things. And besides, I was focused on my own project.

I greeted my friends enthusiastically. Papa Ruzi heard I was visiting and invited me to stay at his house that night. "Argentine, how are things for you and your family in Kitchanga?" he asked softly that evening, even though he already knew the answer. Papa Ruzi often traveled to villages, and he'd already visited me once in Kitchanga, stopping in my atelier and congratulating me. But he knew it was hard, just the way the doctors at the Centre knew our treatment was hard. "Look at you! You're standing," they would say, hoping to give us the strength to go on. Papa Ruzi had congratulated me in the same way. "Look at this atelier! You're doing so good!" he had exclaimed, even though it was clear that I didn't have nearly enough customers.

That evening, as I was visiting the Centre, I told Papa Ruzi my plan. If only I could get a little money, I knew what to do. Papa Ruzi told me to go to his office the next day, and when I went to his office, they gave me fifty dollars for my project.

I stood there with fifty dollars in my hands, and I knew this was my chance. I'd never held that much money in my life. There was no time to return to Kitchanga or to send for one of my brothers to help me. I was on my own, and Virunga Market was waiting for me.

Carefully, I walked out of the Centre on my crutches and called for a motorcycle taxi to carry me to the market. On the edge of the market were women selling used clothes laid out on plastic tarps. I'd seen them on my visits to the market before.

"How much is this coat?" I asked the woman who welcomed me.

"One thousand francs," she answered.

I shook my head thinking of the people back in Kitchanga. No one in Kitchanga could pay a thousand francs for a coat. I pointed in another direction. "What about that shirt?"

"Four hundred francs," she answered.

I sighed in frustration. "How will I ever find anything to bring back to Kitchanga?" I muttered, and the woman had pity on me.

"You must go deep inside the market. That's where they sell vieti," she said, referring to the large bundles of used clothes sold wholesale.

My eyes followed the woman's finger into the market. It was dark and crowded under the tin roof with narrow pathways leading between wooden tables. The ground was covered in rocks and sand. I'd never gone that far into the market before, and I was afraid I would fall. I almost turned back until I thought of how Mama had moved to Kitchanga for me. I thought of how she was still hiking into the fields where soldiers attacked women. I steadied myself on my crutches and turned toward the entrance.

In the heart of the market, I found the used-clothes section. I bought sweaters, shirts and jeans. My pile grew. I called for one of the boys at the market to help me pack all the clothes into a bundle. When I was finished, he carried my bundle to a motorcycle taxi nearby. But when the boy balanced the bundle on the back of the motorcycle taxi, I saw that it was so big there was no place for me to climb on, so I called for a second motorcycle taxi. A crowd was starting to grow around me.

"Ehh, look at this disabled girl. She has enough for two motorcycles!" someone said, and everyone laughed. I flashed a smile back at them. I still had twenty dollars, and I wasn't finished yet.

"Take me to Birere," I told the motorcycle taxi driver, and he drove carefully forward until we arrived in the muddy, crowded streets of Birere—the place where Mama and I had first arrived in Goma.

I found a truck headed to Kitchanga, and a strong man began loading my goods, but I still had one more thing to do. I turned toward a woman sitting at a table by the side of the road. Her table was piled with basins of ground sorghum and sugar. I didn't have enough money to buy the whole basin, so I bought cups of sugar and ground sorghum measured into plastic bags. At another table, I found a woman selling blue, powdery soap, and I bought a few cups of that. Then I bought oil and salt.

I climbed onto the truck beside all my things—ready to return home. As the truck passed through Sake, I barely noticed the soldiers standing hungrily by the side of the road. I was busy thinking about my purchases and calculating the price to put on each item. I'd always dreamt of going to the market, and now I finally had.

When I climbed down from the truck in Kitchanga, I was alone. My family didn't know when I would be returning, so no one had come to meet me. I called to a child nearby and sent him to fetch my brothers. It wasn't ten minutes before my brothers arrived. Their eyes widened and their teeth hung open when they saw the goods piled at my feet.

When we arrived back at the house, my mother looked at me in surprise. "But Argentine, you left here with nothing. How can you have returned with all of this?" she asked. I smiled at her, because it was the same thing I had seen her do all my life.

The next day, Mama did not go out to the fields. Instead, we took the used clothes to the market in Kitchanga. We spread out a tarp on the dirt by the side of the road and laid out each item of clothing.

On the following day, Mama returned to the market to sell more of the clothes, and I returned to the atelier, satisfied that, at least for now, Mama wouldn't have to hike to the fields.

At the atelier, I made space along one wall and asked a boy to build shelves for me. I told my brothers to bring the salt, oil, ground sorghum, sugar, and blue, powdery soap. We divided each into small plastic bags, setting the bags on the shelves for sale, as I had seen Mamí do in Goma. This was my shop, and I was proud. I was finally bringing home the salt and the oil.

Chapter 60

Bunyere and I sang with a youth choir at the Catholic church in Kitchanga. I loved singing with them. "Teach us songs from Goma," the choir members would enthuse, and I would teach them all the newest songs.

One day, the leader of the choir announced that we had been invited to perform in a concert at another church. "We'll spend the night there," the choir leader said, explaining that the church was in Mweso.

"Mweso?" I exclaimed in surprise. "That is the town where I was born!"

"Well, then you must come," my friends answered with excitement.

I thumped my hand on the metal bars of my kinga. "Are you going to push me there in my kinga?" I asked as I laughed. It was 15 kilometers from Kitchanga to Mweso, on a dirt road full of holes. I knew this road. It was the same road I travelled years ago, on top of that towering truck. And even that truck had gotten stuck in the dirt.

"Yes, we will push you!" my friends answered, sincerely.

I kept laughing, picturing me and Bunyere in our kingas with the whole youth choir pushing behind us. I had never imagined that I would return to Mweso, the misty town where Mama and I had stayed with Majinaa. It was a lifetime ago, and I had prayed to never travel that way again. But my choir friends kept insisting that we would travel together.

I sent word back to Shahalia. "Tell everyone that my choir is coming for a concert next weekend in Mweso."

I knew it was a long way from Shahalia to Mweso, a full day's hike across the hills. It was the journey I'd made on the chukudu with Ruberiti, Rupyisi, and Ndahimana. I didn't know if anyone from Shahalia would be able to come all the way to Mweso just to see me. But I knew it was as close as I would get to returning home. *Maybe someone will come to see me,* I thought.

The next week, Bunyere and I traveled the road to Mweso in our kingas, with our choir pushing us forward. We arrived on a Friday night, and on Saturday we held a concert. There were many people, but I didn't see anyone I knew. *It's a very long way for someone to come from Shahalia,* I told myself, looking out at the crowd. Even though I didn't see anyone, I was happy to sing with our choir.

The next day was Sunday. We went to Mass at the church. In the afternoon, we held our second concert. This one was even bigger than the day before. Halfway through the concert, I looked out in the crowd, and there, nudging their way to the front, were Aunt Kampire and two neighbors from Shahalia.

I hadn't known how much I missed my aunt until I saw her generous face and the large circle of hair. I knew that Aunt Kampire had faced many struggles in her life. Uncle Manassé had died from an illness that swept through Shahalia. And then one of their sons had died in a mining accident in Rubaya, a place where the hills were as scarred as my uncle's face. Aunt Kampire was raising her family on her own. She must have been tired. Yet on this day, she had combed her hair into a circle and walked all the way to Mweso to see me.

After the concert, Aunt Kampire rushed toward me. "Argentine, is that truly you?" she said with tears in her eyes. I nodded.

"Can you really stand?" she asked. I was still sitting in my kinga. I snapped my leg braces and hoisted myself on my crutches. Aunt Kampire's whole face lit with joy.

"They've straightened you out! Look how you're standing!" she exclaimed.

"And your teeth are still white!" one of the other neighbors added.

I still couldn't believe these women from Shahalia had come to see me. "Did you walk all the way here?" I asked.

"Yes, Argentine," they answered.

"Just to see me?"

"Yes," Aunt Kampire said, then she continued. "Your mother showed us your photos, but we wanted to see with our own eyes. We wanted to praise God with you."

The next day, our choir would return to Kitchanga, and I knew in my heart that I would never return to Shahalia or Mweso. I might never see these women again. But they had walked this part of the journey with me—and for me. Together we stood and praised God.

Chapter 61

Soon after our youth choir returned to Kitchanga, I started noticing more and more soldiers walking past my atelier. As the soldiers passed by, people sometimes whispered, "Those are Nkunda's soldiers." Other times they whispered, "Those are government soldiers." To me, they all made my skin shake.

One day, one of my friends from the choir walked past my atelier. She had a soldier following behind her. Chantal was younger than me, thirteen or fourteen years old, and I was scared for her.

"Chantal, how are you?" I called out.

"I'm good! I'll come to see you tomorrow! I'll bring my husband," she answered.

"You have a husband?" I cried in surprise.

The next day, Chantal returned with the same man still following behind her. "This is my husband," she said, and I looked at the large man. His face was full from years of eating, and he wore a jacket like a commander. My legs started to shake.

"I want you to sew blouses for the wives of my soldiers," the commander said to me in a low voice. I agreed, trying to sound enthusiastic, but I didn't want to sew for the soldiers or their wives. Who knew if I'd ever be paid? I wanted nothing to do with these men and their guns and their thick, black boots. But I couldn't refuse an order from a commander.

Soldiers' wives started coming into my shop. Some were very young, like Chantal. Others looked tired already. I smiled and sewed for them all, trying to keep my face blank like Mama had taught me.

Sometimes soldiers came without any wives. They came with the soles of their boots flapping open and asked me to sew their boots shut. I felt sorry for them, but they scared me, too.

There was one soldier I liked. He seemed different from the other soldiers. He spoke to me softly, and when he talked, he pulled his lips in and pronounced words strangely. I was sure that something was wrong with his mouth, and I was determined to discover what it was.

"Won't you smile?" I asked him sometimes, and he smiled with his mouth clamped shut. "Are you hungry? Shall I buy you some mandazis?" I offered, hoping to tempt him into opening his mouth. I told jokes hoping to surprise him with laughter, but even when he laughed, he scrunched his lips together, and his hand flew to his face.

"I think he's missing his teeth," I whispered to Mbale, after the soldier left one evening. I could see it in his face. He was like me—missing what should have belonged to him.

Day after day, I kept trying to convince this soldier to open his mouth. "Your lips look so chapped. Let me buy you some milk," I tried one day. It was the first time he ever agreed to drink anything. I sent a boy to bring us mugs of ikivuguto, the thick, sour milk that I loved to drink. I watched the soldier press the mug to his lips, opening them just a sliver. On the edge of his lips, I caught a smile, and we sat there drinking ikivuguto together.

My toothless soldier may have been shy, but I could tell he liked visiting me. He kept returning to sit quietly nearby.

241

Often, he arrived at the end of the day and pushed me in my kinga back to my house.

"Chérie," he said to me one day, "will you be my wife?"

"Ohhhhhh," I said, "I could never be a soldier's wife. Your life is too hard and too full of secrets. From one day to the next, you don't know where you will go, or if you will return."

I thought about it that night. I liked my toothless soldier, and I wanted a husband and children. But I knew many soldiers' wives. I'd seen how one day they would be walking proudly down the streets of Kitchanga, and the next day they would be scrambling down the road to follow their husbands, dragging children and mattresses with them.

And I had seen the wives who stayed behind, who sent their husbands off one day and stood waiting for them to return. Sometimes, those soldiers never came home, and their wives were left with nothing.

"I could never be a soldier's wife," I said tentatively to my mother, hoping she would disagree. But my mother looked back at me, her eyes round with horror.

"No! No!" she said. "That can't be the life for you!"

My toothless soldier kept visiting me though. "Chérie," he said, "I will stop this life of soldiering. I'll throw my guns in the forest, and we can run away to my family in Minova."

I thought about it. But I knew that soldiers never stop soldiering. "You can't leave," I said sadly. "They'll find you, wherever you go."

The days continued like that with my toothless soldier dreaming of a different life, while I was still wondering how he had lost his teeth. He was a young man, and there were no scars on his face—no story of what had been done to him. I tried to ask clever questions that led me in circles.

"Before you became a soldier, were you healthy?" I asked. "Did you ever get in a fight?"

He shook his head. I could never ask the question directly. I couldn't ask him what happened to his teeth any more than he could ask what happened to my legs. At the Centre, they always told us never to ask. "People have to choose to share those stories," they instructed.

Sometimes, my toothless soldier disappeared for days or weeks at a time. But then he'd return. When he returned, I'd ask suspiciously, "Did you go off to fight?"

And he would reassure me, "No, no. They didn't send me to war. I just went somewhere else."

But he was a soldier. And soldiers go off to fight.

Chapter 62

My friend, Chantal, seemed to be happy as a commander's wife. I often saw her walking down the main road. Sometimes she'd stop, and we'd laugh and gossip together. One day, as I sat in front of my sewing machine, she leaned toward me and lowered her voice. "My husband wants to see you."

My heart flew out of my stomach. I didn't want to go, but I couldn't say that.

In the afternoon, Espoir, pushed me over to the commander's house. He lived in a stone house with lines of soldiers and trucks parked out front. As I drew closer, I could see the commander distributing bags of beans and containers of oil to the soldiers. He called me over.

Maybe he'll ask me to sew more blouses, I thought dejectedly. I'd never been paid for the ones I had sewn, but I wasn't going to mention that. I'd sew however many blouses the commander asked for, if only he would leave me alone.

The commander gestured toward one of the soldiers, and they started loading oil and beans into my kinga. I watched in silence. He was paying me for the blouses I'd sewn—paying me in rations, like I was a soldier. I was thankful. Our family needed all the food we could find.

Everyone in our family did whatever we could to bring food to the house. When there were no clothes to sell, my mother still trekked out to the fields to farm. My father and Tera had started pushing a chukudu loaded with banana beer from one village to another. It was heavy work. The wooden scooter was loaded with three twenty-liter containers, and they had to push it up and down steep slopes. If they ran into soldiers along the way, they'd return home with nothing.

Whenever I had money, I traveled to the market in Goma to buy more used clothing for Mama to sell. I started bringing Tera with me. The first time I brought him, Tera watched quietly from the minibus, his eyes growing wide as we came down the winding road and stopped at the barrier in Sake.

When we arrived in Goma, we went to the market and piled clothes into a bundle. Tera carried the bundle over to the motorcycle taxis.

I looked at Tera's eager face and whispered to him, "You ride with me." I was unwilling to let my brother out of my sight. He didn't look like a city child. I was sure someone would rob him.

On the way home, Tera and I talked about the future. "After you learn how to do all of this, you can teach Espoir," I advised. "The two of you can do it together."

But that never happened. On our next journey there were more roadblocks. Our bus was stopped by soldiers making demands. I tried not to look at them, or their boots, or their guns. I had heard about people being beaten and killed, and boys being forced into the pori to fight.

As I sat on the plastic seat, I looked nervously over at Tera's face. He was still a village boy—my little brother. And these roads were dangerous for boys. What if the soldiers stole him away? What if they forced him into the pori to fight? How would I explain that to Mama?

It was too dangerous. No matter how much I wanted to go to the market, this was too much. Tera and I stopped traveling the road to Goma.

Chapter 63

When I first arrived in Kitchanga, people talked about war, but it was always happening somewhere else. Now, it began to arrive at our door. I heard bullets crying in the night. I hated that sound. It reminded me of Shahalia. Soon, there were bullets crying even in daylight. The soldiers in the streets multiplied.

"What kind of soldier is Nkunda?" I asked, before I remembered to circle my tongue. People said he was a rebel. They said he was fighting for the Tutsis who lived in the hills. Slowly, I came to understand that he and his soldiers had been part of the peace accords in 2003, while I was still at the Centre. They had joined the government army for a while, but now he was leading his own rebel movement again.

"What does he want?" I asked.

"He wants to be president of our country," someone said, and after I heard that response, I closed my heart and decided not to ask any more questions.

One day, I heard that General Nkunda had called a meeting on the main road in Kitchanga by the round point. I did not go to my atelier that day. But later that evening, my father brought news of the meeting. He told us that Nkunda's soldiers had their own national anthem now.

"But we already have a national anthem," I said, thinking of the days I went to school in Shahalia, and we sang "Debout Congolais."

My father gave me his radio and told me to listen for myself. The next morning, I turned on that radio. To start the day, they always played the national anthem. But this time it wasn't "Debout Congolais." It was a new song with new voices. I stared at the radio as the song filled my heart with terror. I knew one country could not have two national anthems.

Chapter 64

I heard that many of Nkunda's soldiers were returning to Kitchanga with terrible injuries. "They're filling the hospital," a neighbor explained.

I wanted to see those soldiers for myself. I wanted to count their legs like I wanted to count the teeth of my toothless soldier. We can only mourn for what we can see. This was the lesson of Onze Onze all over again. I was determined to visit whoever was suffering, even if they were soldiers.

I cooked a meal of beans and cabbage, bought orange Fanta and fresh papayas, and asked Espoir to push me over to the hospital. As we neared the building, I started to wonder if this was such a good idea, but it was too late to turn back. Outside the hospital was a soldier with his arm in a sling.

"Who have you come to see?" he demanded harshly.

"No one," I mumbled. "I don't know anyone."

The soldier stood there looking at me in confusion.

"I've come to see whoever is hurt," I added.

The soldier looked at the pots in my kinga. "This food you've brought, is it for anyone?" he asked.

"Yes, anyone who needs it."

The soldier softened his voice. "Sister, you can come in."

In front of me was a step, and there was no way I could enter with my kinga, so the soldier offered his good arm and helped me stand with my crutches.

Inside, there were many soldiers. All of them were silent, lying flat on their backs, in rows of wooden beds. It was like the Centre. In one bed there was a boy whose body was so small that he couldn't have been more than twelve years old. He was Espoir's age. But he was a soldier. I saw it in his face.

I gave the soldiers—the sick people—everything I had. They ate the food and drank the Fanta in silence. The air was heavy, and it smelled of sickness. No one had anything to say. After they ate, they thanked me, and I left. When I walked out the doors of that hospital, I hated Kitchanga. I hated this place where all the boys wore uniforms and came home with no legs.

For weeks, I kept thinking about those soldiers. My heart was torn. They were strangers. They could have been anyone. They could have been the men who burned villages—who fell on women—who held knives to little boys' stomachs.

But they also could have been the boys who were caught pushing chukudus on the road alone—stolen from villages and forced to fight. They could have been my brothers. And now they were disabled like me.

Chapter 65

I hadn't seen my toothless soldier for a long time. Every day, I sat outside my sewing shop, hoping he would return. But he never did. And in his absence, other soldiers started leaning too close.

One morning a tall soldier stopped in front of my atelier. I could feel his eyes running over me.

"It's you again," he said. "Don't you remember me?"

I didn't remember him, but he explained how he'd walked past our house the other day. I didn't want to talk to this soldier, and I didn't like the way he was looking at me. I wanted to go home, but it was clear that he already knew where I lived.

The tall soldier settled into a chair and called for a boy to bring him a beer from a shop nearby. I wished he was my toothless soldier who only drank milk. But this soldier was nothing like my friend. I could see all his teeth as he noisily swallowed his beer and smacked his lips.

Nervously, I turned my head to make sure Mbale was still beside me. She was sitting in front of her sewing machine, spinning her handle in circles and pretending to sew as her eyes grew bigger and bigger.

"I like you. I want to marry you," the tall soldier said to me. His eyes were shining.

"Oh no, I can't marry a soldier," I answered right away, but he didn't seem to hear me at all.

"I'll build you a house in the hills. You can be mine. All mine," he continued.

"No, I can't do that," I insisted, horrified at the thought of being carried high into the hills.

The soldier stood to leave. "Don't be afraid," he said as he smiled. "One day I'll come with a truck and carry you and your kinga away."

All these years, Mama had been trying to keep me safe, and now I had stumbled right into danger. What had I done? Why had I been sitting on the main road where anyone could find me?

I didn't tell Mama, but soon she heard the news for herself. One day, she came rushing into my atelier. "I saw a soldier in the street," she stammered. "He said you're his wife."

I tried to calm her. "He's probably drunk," I dismissed.

But Mama looked straight into my eyes. "Argentine, he is going to come and steal you away. You must leave Kitchanga."

Mama was right. It wasn't safe for me in Kitchanga. But what could I do? Kitchanga was a rebel town now, cut off from everywhere else. I didn't think there were any minibuses traveling to Goma anymore.

I was so scared of the tall soldier that I stopped going to my atelier on the main road. Instead, I stayed in our house. But one day the tall soldier arrived at our house, thumping his fist on the door. There was no way to hide. He could see my kinga outside, and he knew I was there.

"I want to speak to you and your mother together," he said, promising to return that Thursday. I knew it would be a proposal—one that I couldn't refuse.

That night my mind spun looking for a solution. My thoughts ran faster and faster. *I'll pretend to be sick,* I thought. *He can't bother me if I am sick.*

That Thursday, I didn't leave my bed. When the tall soldier arrived, Mama opened the door and announced that I was sick. "Maybe you can come back some other day," she offered.

But the tall soldier pushed his way inside, demanding to see me.

Lying in bed, I felt his breath above me. He touched the blankets. "I'm going to take her to the hospital," he announced.

This was a terrible plan, I realized.

I heard Mama clear her throat. "Can you fetch some medicine first?" she suggested. The tall soldier agreed.

As soon as he was gone, my eyes flew open, and I pushed the blanket off me.

"Stay there," Mama warned. "He's going to come back, and you can't be standing up."

I got back under the blanket. "Whatever you do, don't let him carry me out of this house," I begged. It wasn't long before the soldier returned bearing medicine. Mama propped me up, and I drank the medicine as the tall soldier hovered nearby. The next day he returned with more medicine.

"What else can I bring?" he asked.

"Bring her some milk," Mama suggested.

The following day he brought milk and more medicine. He kept asking if I was getting better and threatening to take me to the hospital. I stayed in bed, but our excuses were vanishing like water on a hot day. I knew that one day this soldier would come and take me away.

Then, one day, he didn't come. I breathed in relief. *Maybe he's tired of me*, I thought. But after a few days, a group of soldiers arrived. When we heard the knock on the door, I scrambled into bed and pretended to be sick again. The soldiers looked at me lying in bed and said they brought bad news. "Your fiancé had to go away for a time," they explained.

My heart burst into relief. I tried to keep my face blank like a rock. I was free.

As they were leaving, one of the soldiers turned back toward me. "Don't worry, your fiancé will return. He won't forget you. He'll come for you soon."

Chapter 66

The next morning, I looked at the path in front of our house and found it strangely empty. It reminded me of that day in Goma, when the sun didn't shine, and grey specks fell from the sky—the day when all the people disappeared.

After a few minutes, I saw a neighbor outside of his house. I called out a greeting, and he rushed over, trying to hush me.

"What are you doing outside? They're fighting nearby," he warned, then ran back to his own house.

Later that afternoon, my father came home and told me that people were running. "They're going to MONUC," he said, referring to a peacekeeping base nearby. My father offered to push me there in my kinga, but the thought of being stuck in a crowd terrified me. I remembered Da Georgette, with her fine kikwembe, her powdered cheeks, and her metal braces that squeaked when she walked. When the volcano erupted, Da Georgette's family had tried to push her to safety, but she had never made it. I didn't want my family to try and push me anywhere.

"What if the fighting arrives at MONUC?" I asked my father.

"The peacekeepers will fight back," he answered. "If it gets bad, maybe they'll carry everyone out in an airplane."

I nodded my head doubtfully. The MONUC soldiers had arrived in cars and trucks, not airplanes, and I knew what would happen if MONUC was attacked. We'd have to run again.

"I'll stay in the house," I said.

I was stuck like a tongue between teeth. I couldn't run, and I couldn't hide. Kitchanga wasn't like Shahalia. There were no banana stalks outside our house where Mama could hide me. The only thing outside our house was a swamp, and past the swamp was the pori where bullets were crying.

"You can't stay here," Mama said.

"Let us push you in your kinga back to Goma," Ushindi piped up. He was only ten years old. I tried to imagine my brothers pushing me in my kinga eighty-five kilometers back to Goma on a road that was no longer safe for minibuses to travel. Even if I survived, my brothers would be carried off to the pori to fight.

Suddenly, I was overwhelmed by the risk my brothers were taking. I knew even small children were kidnapped and turned into soldiers. And here my brothers were stuck in our house in Kitchanga because of me. They would have run if I wasn't there. Mama and baby Aline would have run. I was the one endangering us all.

That's when I knew what I had to do. I had to leave. It was the only way I could protect my family. I thought of my mother on top of that hill called Gapfura. I thought of the way that she hid us under branches then turned away, preparing to climb back down the hill and into danger. "If I don't go, we'll starve," she had told us.

What kind of faith had that taken? What kind of love? She must have believed that God would protect us.

My mother never told us what she saw on those trips down the hill. We never knew the dangers she faced. We only knew that she never forgot us. She always came back calling our names.

Now, it was my turn to go.

Chapter 67

There were no buses traveling between Kitchanga and Goma anymore, but I thought maybe I could find a Fuso. Surely, the people of Goma still needed potatoes and onions and sorghum from Masisi. The next day, I convinced my brothers to push me to the place where strong men packed trucks.

At last, we found one Fuso going to Goma. It was loaded high with sacks of crops—too high. I tilted my head and stared at the top of the truck. I could see people sitting up there. I didn't want to sit up there. I knew that my back would wobble like porridge, but I took a deep breath and calmed my fears. This was my chance to follow my mother's example. I had to leave Kitchanga before something terrible happened to us all.

Someone hoisted me onto the truck, and I pressed myself between the shoulders of strangers. The road ahead frightened me, but I closed my heart and prayed for my family. I prayed one day we'd all be together again.

The Fuso swayed forward, and soon we stopped at a roadblock. I heard voices shouting, but I was so high that I could see nothing except sky.

The truck swayed. We were turning around. "They're returning us to Kitchanga," the man next to me said. Everyone started shaking their heads and sucking their teeth as our Fuso moved back toward Kitchanga. The road was cut, and there was no way forward.

When I returned to Kitchanga, I was more discouraged than ever.

"Don't worry, Nkunda's soldiers will protect us," some of our neighbors predicted. But others started whispering that the government would start bombing Kitchanga soon.

When I was at the Centre, unable to walk, I'd lie in bed with my thoughts racing faster and faster, as though my mind could make up for what my body lacked. Now my head was spinning again, considering every possible way to leave Kitchanga. I couldn't stay in this place anymore.

There was only one kind of person who still traveled the road from Kitchanga to Goma, and that was a soldier. My toothless soldier had never returned, but he couldn't have helped me anyway. He was only a boy. I needed someone stronger. I knew only one commander—the man that Chantal had married.

I hadn't seen Chantal in a while because I never left the house anymore. But I tried to remember every single interaction that I had with Chantal and her husband. I had said only good things. I had watched my words carefully, circling my tongue seven times as Mama had taught me. And now, that mattered more than anything else.

This commander was my only chance.

Chapter 68

I began to form a plan. First, I asked Espoir to push me in my kinga to the atelier. He looked at me, startled. I hadn't been to the atelier in months—ever since the tall soldier started visiting me there. Now, with the bullets crying, sitting out on the main road was the last place anyone wanted to be. But I nodded my head confidently at Espoir, and he pushed my kinga through the deserted streets. When we arrived at the shop, I told him to pull my sewing table outside.

"You want to sew, now?" he asked, even more confused.

"Yes," I answered, without any further explanation.

I was open for business, but there was only one customer I wanted to see. I sat there all day waiting for Chantal to pass, like a cat waiting to pounce. Soon, she walked across the road with her son tied to her back.

"Argentine! Is that you?" she asked when she saw me. "Where have you been?"

"I have been sick," I offered. What else could I say? I couldn't say that I was terrified of a soldier. Her husband was a commander.

"I've been feeling very poorly," I said.

"But you're feeling better now?" Chantal asked, and I nodded. "So, when are you going to sew me a dress?" she teased.

That was my opening. I invited Chantal to come the next day so that I could measure her and her son. "I'll sew for you both," I promised.

The next day, she returned. I waited until my measuring tape was already pressed to her body, then I tried a question. "How is your husband?" I asked as casually as I could. "Does he still travel the road to Goma?"

"Sometimes..." Chantal answered vaguely.

I took a breath. "There is something I want to talk to your husband about."

"Oh, yes? What is it?" Chantal asked.

I started talking—drawing pictures with my words. I told Chantal how my leg braces were broken, and I needed to go back to the Centre to have them fixed. I told her how my back had been hurting, and I needed the doctors at the Centre to make a brace for me. I went on and on with all the reasons I needed to return to Goma. I said nothing about war. I said nothing about soldiers. I gave her only the words that she needed to hear.

Chantal seemed to be counting in her head, calculating something.

"I don't know if my husband can agree to take you to Goma," she said doubtfully.

But then she looked in my eyes. We both understood what neither of us was saying. She knew that Kitchanga wasn't safe for me. It probably wasn't safe for her either.

"Here's what we'll do," Chantal said quickly. "Sew me this dress, and I will start preparing my husband. When the dress is ready, you'll have a reason to come to our house and talk to my husband."

I stayed at the shop all day sewing Chantal's clothing as quickly as I could. The next morning Chantal walked by my atelier again. "My husband's home," she whispered. "He's meeting with people. Come in your kinga and wait for him outside."

I hid my hands under the sewing table so Chantal wouldn't see them shaking. I had never asked anything of a soldier before, especially not a commander. What might he ask of me in return?

Espoir pushed me over to Chantal's stone house. There were soldiers outside. They looked at me curiously. My heart started to pound. I hated those uniforms and boots and the way their hats hid their faces.

The commander walked out the door. "Sister Argentine! There you are! My wife told me that you sewed her some clothing. I'll pay you next week," he said, and started to turn away from me.

"Oh, don't worry about that," I called out. "But wait, there is one thing I was hoping to talk to you about..."

The commander turned back toward me. I knew that Chantal had already told him how I needed to go to Goma. "But he wants to hear it from you," she had instructed.

"Commandant, I need to go to Goma," I started.

He lifted his eyebrows. "But why do you want to leave us here in Kitchanga? Aren't my soldiers keeping you safe?"

"Oh yes! They are keeping us safe!" I answered enthusiastically. "Only...I need to go to the Centre Pour Handicapés," I said, and quickly added, "I will come right back." I showed him my leg braces and my back. I talked and talked about my disability.

Finally, the commander stopped me. "Are you sure you will return?"

"Oh yes, Commandant. I will return very soon," I promised.

He looked at me with a blank expression. I don't know if he believed me or not.

"I'll take you," he said finally. Then he leaned forward and added, "But you can't bring anyone or anything with you. You must come on your own, and you must leave everything you have behind."

Chapter 69

The next week, on a cold, misty morning, I said goodbye to my family. I still wasn't sure if this commander was really going to help me. I'd already tried to leave once and failed. I wasn't sure if I'd ever succeed.

I left my sewing machine with Mama, telling her to sell it if she could. On my waist, I wrapped one kikwembe and then another. I did the same with my shirts. I was wearing layers of clothing, the same way we did at night in Shahalia, ready to run with whatever we had. My layers of clothing were the only possessions that I could take with me.

Espoir pushed me in my kinga over to the commander's house. We arrived early in the morning and waited outside. When the commander finally walked out of his door, Espoir left, pushing the kinga. There could be no goodbyes.

The commander led me over to a small vehicle with an open top, like a jeep. My heart left my stomach. It was a military vehicle—painted green. I would be traveling like a soldier.

The commander turned to me and studied my clothing carefully. "If anyone asks who you are, say you are my daughter. Don't say anything else."

I promised to follow his instructions.

"Listen, you know that I can't take you all the way to Goma, right? I have to stop at the barrier in Sake," the commander explained.

"Yes Commandant," I answered, trying to look confident, even though this journey kept getting worse. First, I could bring nothing and no one. Next, I was traveling in a military vehicle. And now, I was going to be abandoned in Sake, the town with the swamp and the hungry soldiers—the town where no one wanted to spend the night. I'd be at the mercy of those soldiers. I was like a beast of the forest again, running without knowing where I was going.

Only God could help me now.

I climbed into the commander's small vehicle. All these years, I had been fleeing from soldiers, and now here I was traveling beside one. The commander started the engine. As we picked up speed, the cold wind rushed through me, and I started to shake.

Soon we reached a checkpoint with men holding guns. I squeezed my eyes shut like I was a child again. The commander announced, "This is my daughter. I am taking her to the hospital." The men with guns started talking between themselves. My heart left my body just as it had on the day the volcano erupted. After some time, we started moving again. The cold air cut through me like a machete.

I don't know how many checkpoints we stopped at. The road was curvy and steep. I felt dizzy. Finally, we arrived at the outskirts of Sake. I saw the swamp where people said that soldiers threw bodies.

Our vehicle stopped, and the commander looked at me inquisitively. "Are you well?" he asked, and I nodded. "I have to leave you here," he said. "This is Sake. The barrier is ahead."

I wished the commander could stay with me. I didn't want to be left by the side of the road any more than I wanted to be left on top of a hill.

The commander interrupted my thoughts. "Do you have enough money for the bus ticket to Goma?" he asked.

"Yes, Commandant," I answered.

I had francs tucked in a piece of fabric I'd sewn under my clothes, and I didn't want to ask for anything more from this man who had unexpectedly saved my life. He'd done nothing but help me, and I had to let him go.

I thanked the commander and said goodbye. He turned his vehicle around and sped back the way we had come. I climbed on a bicycle taxi that carried me to the checkpoint.

At the checkpoint, I stood on my crutches. I could almost feel Mama Vero's hand on my back. I remembered the first time I'd stood at the parallel bars—the way everyone clapped like mothers watching a baby stand. I threw my legs forward and started to move. Slowly, I crossed the checkpoint. The soldiers didn't say anything to me.

After I crossed the barrier in Sake, I found a minibus going to Goma. We passed white tents, wooden shacks, and grey rock walls. I saw tall poles and wires strung like ropes from one house to the next. I saw women selling corn by the side of the road. As I watched the world outside my window, my heart started to return to my stomach. We were arriving in Goma, and it felt familiar.

When we reached the neighborhood of Birere, our minibus stopped. I slid from my seat, snapped my leg braces, and hoisted myself onto my crutches again. This time I didn't feel so wobbly.

I had returned to Goma.

I had survived.

"Mungu asifiwe. God be praised," I said as a song rose in my heart. *Mungu wetu wa ajabu, ajabu, ajabu. Our God of wonders, wonders, wonders.*

In front of me, I could see the streets filled with black oily mud and dirty plastic bags. This was Birere—the same neighborhood I'd crawled as a child when Mama and I first arrived in Goma. This was the place I'd gotten lost.

But I knew that I wasn't lost anymore. In my mind, I saw the faces of all the people who'd carried me this far. They were right there beside me—they'd been there the whole time. I saw Aunt Kampire again, like I'd seen her at the concert in Mweso. I saw Uncle Manassé squatting beside me, a piece of fruit tucked behind his back. I saw my mother carrying her children like a cat and Bébé carrying me through the rain. I saw an old man with one leg, praying as the volcano erupted. I saw Sister Louise and Mama Pastor and so many people whose names I will never know.

All of them had carried me part of the way.

As a child, I went to church with my grandfather, and I sang a song like a prayer. *"May I not go alone. May I not go alone."* This was God's answer to me. This was his miracle–I had never walked alone. God had always sent someone to walk with me part of the way.

As I stood on my crutches in the crowded streets of Goma, I wasn't scared anymore. I knew that I would find more friends up ahead. Someone would offer me a place to live. I'd find a sewing shop where I could work. It wouldn't be easy, but I'd start earning money again.

As soon as I could, I would send help back to my family in Kitchanga. I'd send money for charcoal. I'd buy an old motorcycle for Tera to use as a taxi. I'd pay for Espoir to intern at a beauty salon in Goma. I'd bring my little sister, Aline, to live with me. I'd send help to Bunyere and Shayo and anyone that I could.

My thoughts were filled with a future I could finally see. I still didn't know all the places I'd go. I didn't even know where I'd sleep that night.

But I knew who I would be.

I would be just like my mother. Just like Ruberiti, Rupyisi and Ndahimana. Just like all the people who carried me part of the way.

I'd go wherever I had to go, and I'd carry whoever I could.

Until one day, we'd meet in this grocery store in Canada, where the air is cold, and the avocados cost two dollars each. And I'd tell you this story about the people I love—because they are my family—and so are you.

And we are all walking together.

Epilogue

Argentine remained in Goma for five years. Initially, she worked at a restaurant where she was paid only with food. Later, she found an opportunity to begin sewing again, and she started sending money back to her mother in Kitchanga. With that money, Argentine's mother was able to buy charcoal for their family instead of hiking into the hills to search for firewood. To this day, Argentine's mother speaks with pride about that change in her life.

Argentine brought her brother, Espoir, to Goma, arranging an internship for him at a small beauty shop. She bought a motorcycle for Tera to use as a taxi, so that he could stop pushing the chukudu loaded with banana beer. And she helped raise her sister, Aline, bringing her to Goma when she was only five years old.

During this time, Argentine formed a small sewing group called SHONA Congo along with Mapendo Ndongotsi and Dawn Hurley. Later, Riziki and Solange joined the group. This small sewing group helped connect Argentine with customers around the globe, creating connections that would later prove lifesaving. You can read about this part of Argentine's life in our first book, *The Place Between Our Fears*.

In 2009, Laurent Nkunda was placed under house arrest in Rwanda, and his rebel group, the CNDP, signed a peace agreement and agreed to integrate into the Congolese army. Three years later, many of those troops defected again creating another Rwandan-backed rebel group called the M23.

In 2012, the M23 attacked the city of Goma, causing many people, including Argentine, Mapendo, Riziki, and Solange to flee. Friends of SHONA Congo supported the women as they fled to refugee camps in Burundi and later Uganda.

In 2017, Argentine and Mapendo, along with their families, were sponsored for resettlement in Cananda through the Athabasca Interfaith Refugee Sponsorship Society. This was made possible through connections from SHONA Congo and support from friends around the globe. It was also made possible by every single person who carried Argentine part of the way, from Shahalia to Mweso to Goma and beyond.

In 2022, Argentine's brother, Espoir, was also sponsored for resettlement in Canada by AIRSS.

In 2025, the M23 rebels escalated attacks throughout eastern Congo, forcing families out of their homes and out of camps where they had been seeking safety.

Also, in 2025, on his first day in office, President Trump suspended indefinitely the entire refugee resettlement program of the United States. Weeks later, President Trump halted funding for US humanitarian assistance around the globe, causing a sudden cut in programs that provide water, food, and medicine to displaced people. Conditions in eastern Congo remain extremely difficult, with over 7 million people internally displaced and fighting ongoing. As Eglantyne Jebb famously said, "Every war is a war against children."

When considering her life, Argentine often shakes her head in wonder. She says, "If only people could see where I came from, they'd understand that with God's grace anything is possible." We offer Argentine's story in this spirit of hope.

Anything is possible—if we choose to carry each other.

***

On one occasion an expert in the law stood up to test Jesus. "Teacher," he asked, "what must I do to inherit eternal life?"

"What is written in the Law?" Jesus replied. "How do you read it?"

He answered, "'Love the Lord your God with all your heart and with all your soul and with all your strength and with all your mind'; and 'Love your neighbor as yourself.'"

"You have answered correctly," Jesus replied. "Do this and you will live."

But the man wanted to justify himself, so he asked Jesus, "And who is my neighbor?"

Luke 10:25-29

***

Home

"no one leaves home unless
home is the mouth of a shark
you only run for the border
when you see the whole city running as well..."
~"Home" by Warsan Shire

❖ Argentine's parents live as refugees in Uganda, along with Tera, Ushindi, Soleil, and Argentine's youngest sister, Pascaline (born after the end of this book's timeline). Argentine's assistance allowed the family to flee to safety in Uganda.

❖ Argentine, Espoir and Aline live in Canada. Together, they send help back to their family in Uganda. Their help provides crucial food, medicine, education, and housing for their family.

❖ Argentine is the very proud mother of three children. Her oldest child, Rachelle, died while they were in Congo. Her younger children, AsanteMungu and Jean ByaMungu, live with her in Canada.

❖ Aunt Kampire was forced to flee from her home in Shahalia in 2022. She now lives with her daughter, Sifa, Argentine's childhood playmate.

- Sifa and her children live in Kitchanga on the land that Argentine's family left behind. Argentine sent money to Sifa to rebuild the house.

- Argentine's friend, Shayo, lives in a refugee camp in Uganda. Friends of SHONA bought her a sewing machine and cloth.

- Bunyere lives in a refugee camp in Burundi with her daughter, Davina. They fled Kitchanga in 2022. Argentine sends help to her friends whenever she can.

- Chantal lives in Goma with five children.

- Riziki and Solange remain in Goma with their children despite enormously difficult conditions. Argentine helps them sell their handcrafted work. You can buy their work at our website, www.shonacongo.com.

Shukrani

Thank you to our SHONA Congo friends. Thank you for your faith, your patience, and your constant support.

Thank you to our thoughtful editor, Damien Pitter, our proof-reader, Catriona Turner, and our cover designer, Laura Duffy.

Thank you to Cheryl Balay. We are grateful for your endless dedication and your eagle eyes.

Special thanks to our families. We love you.

Get involved.

www.shonacongo.com

www.ingramcontent.com/pod-product-compliance
Lightning Source LLC
Chambersburg PA
CBHW021710120626
46545CB00004B/1495